THE CANARY ISLANDS MIGRATION TO LOUISIANA 1778-1783

The history and passenger lists of the Islenos volunteer recruits and their families

Compiled and written
By
Sidney Louis Villeré

CLEARFIELD

Originally Published
Genealogical Research Society of New Orleans
New Orleans, 1971

Reprinted with Permission of the Author
Genealogical Publishing Co., Inc.
Baltimore, 1972

Reprinted for
Clearfield Company, Inc. by
Genealogical Publishing Co., Inc.
Baltimore, Maryland
1997

Library of Congress Cataloging in Publication Data
Villeré, Sidney Louis.
The Canary Islands migration to Louisiana, 1778-1783.
1. Louisiana—Emigration and immigration. 2. Canary Islands—Emigration and immigration. 3. Louisiana—Genealogy. I. Title.
[F368.V54 1972] 929'.3763 72-7239
ISBN 0-8063-0522-3

Made in the United States of America

Introduction

Prior to 1778, Louisiana, then a Spanish Province, was severely restricted in her commerce with foreign nations. This was pursuant to the drastic edicts which emanated from the Royal Court and which confined trade only to vessels owned and commanded by Spanish subjects and which sailed exclusively from six home ports, namely:

> Seville, Alicante, Malaga, Carthagena,
> Barcelona and Corunna.

1778 was the year in which these severe restrictions were lifted. Spain then adopted more moderate and progressive measures which had their effect upon her colonies at the precise time that certain settlements were being founded in Louisiana. The King of Spain, Don Carlos III, shipped to the Province of Louisiana, at his own expense, a large number of agriculturists among whom were soldiers. These were mainly volunteers who were recruited from the Canary Islands by officers sent from the Spanish colonies for that purpose. As an inducement, the Spanish Crown had offered each volunteer a home, tools, and the means of subsistence for at least four years. A church was to be placed in a central location where all could assemble and pray.

Sails Unfurled To The West

The Canary Islanders migrated to Louisiana between the years 1778-1783. They were called "islenos", and their ancestral domain was a chain of small islands about sixty five miles west of the African coast, and southwest of the Spanish peninsular. They were members of the white race, and spoke a native Portuguese dialect. In 1492, the great discoverer, Christopher Columbus, had anchored his sturdy ships at the Canaries en route to the New World. Now they also, were to set sail to the fabled country which gave them promise of a better livelihood.

The Spanish ships that played such an historic role in the migration of the Canary Islanders to the Province of Louisiana were as follows:

SS Sacremento
San Ignacio de Loyola
La Victoria
San Juan Nepomuceno
La Santa Faz
El Sagrada Corazon de Jesus
Fragata Llamada Margarita
SS Trinadad.

A few of these ships sailed to Vera Cruz and Havana before reaching New Orleans, for additional supplies and personnel were needed to accomplish the success of the migration. As the respective vessels arrived periodically to unload their freight and passengers near the "Plaza d'Armas," it can be assumed that Don Bernardo de Galvez and other Spanish officials of the Cabildo were on hand to make note of the volunteer recruits. The "islenos" were immediately classified for expediency. Soldier recruits enrolled among several Spanish regiments for training. Agriculturists, women and children were conveyed to the respective settlements promised to them.

Settlement Foundations

The villages allocated to the Canary Islanders were as follows:

"San Bernardo de Galvez", located on the shores of the Terre-Aux-Boeuf in Saint Bernard Parish.

"Galveztown", located on the shores of the Amite river near Manchac, in Iberville Parish.

"Valenzuela", located on the shores of the Chetimachas (Bayou Lafourche), in Assumption Parish.

"Nueva Iberia", located on the shores of the Bayou Teche in Iberia Parish.

Louisiana's American Revolution

On May 8, 1779, Don Carlos III, King of Spain, formally declared war on England, and she pooled her efforts with France in North America to help the hard-pressed Americans in their war of independence. Don Bernado de Galvez jumped into the campaign with enthusiasm, as he was young and ambitious. On July 13, 1779, he conveyed at New Orleans his War Council ("Junta de Guerra"), and asked them to submit a plan of attack. Accordingly, to the "Plaza del Cabildo" the members of the War Council arrived to debate their views. They were namely:

Colonel Manuel Gonzalez
Lieutenant Colonel Estevan Miro
Lieutenant Colonel Pedro Piernas
Captain Martin Mozun
Captain Francisco Cruzat
Captain Alesandro Coussot
Captain Manuel de Nava
Captain Hilario de Estenoy
Captain Juan de la Villebeuvre
Captain Joaquin de Blanca
Captain Pedro Josef Favrot
Captain Jacinto Panis, acting as Secretary.

The militia officials urged Galvez to wait for reinforcements from Havana before launching an offensive. But the Governor was not a man to bide his time. In a remarkably short period, the glorious campaigns against the English at Natchez, Manchac, Baton Rouge, Mobile and Pensacola, became a part of the documented history of our country. And in the campaign that followed, the newly-arrived "islenos" soldiers were able to repay Spain the small pittance extended to their respective families by their exemplary conduct during the War of the American Revolution.

Valenzuela

"Valenzuela" and "Galveztown" were established to accomodate American and Canadian Colonials who, upon fulfilling the legal requirements ordered by the Spanish Crown, could seek a domicile there.

"Valenzuela", at the time of the Canary Island migration there, was situated near the present-day "Belle Alliance Plantation." The descendants of the "islenos" settlers now comprise a considerable part of the indigenous population of Assumption and Ascension Parishes. They built their modest huts on the banks of the "Chetimachas", which was name of a regional Indian tribe. Today the stream is known as "Bayou Lafourche." Their first Captain-Commandant was Nicolas Verret, Sr., who in turn was succeeded by Don Martin de Villanueva y Barroso.

Galveztown

Don Bernardo de Galvez in a report to his government on January 15, 1779, stated that he had discovered the site of "Galveztown" quite by chance. It was a site of high land near the junction of the Amite and Iberville rivers. Bayou Manchac in the 18th century was called "Iberville River." It was at the site of "Galveztown" that the Americans and their English sympathizers had fled to seek refuge in the domaines of the King of Spain. They formed a village and named it "Galveztown" as a mark of gratitude to the Governor under whom they had found protection.

When the Spanish government embarked upon the task of colonizing its newly acquired Province of Louisiana with Spaniards, "Galveztown" was one of the first locations to draw the attention of the Spanish authorities. The move to "Galveztown" was a clever one for the Spanish officials, as the new settlement acted as a "buffer zone" to Manchac, an English military and mercantile post on the extreme southwestern corner of the modern Parish of East Baton Rouge. The English ascendancy had steadily increased since the cession of the two Floridas to Great Britain. But Spain could not have selected a more unfit set of colonists to Hispanize: Spain's sincere intent in bringing the "islenos" to the province was to safeguard and increase the prestige of the Catholic monarchy.

Don Francisco Maxilmillien de Saint Maxent was the first Captain-Commandant at "Galveztown". He was the son of the wealthy and controversial Don Gilberto Antonio de Saint Maxent of New Orleans. After a short tenure in office, Saint Maxent the son, was despatched for official duties in New Orleans, and he was then replaced by Don Francisco Collel.

By 1786, Saint Maxent resumed his duties at "Galveztown." As trade was monopolized by the Americans and English who had fled their mother-country, the "islenos" were helplessly at their mercy. Consequently here at "Galveztown" the "islenos" did not lay the foundations of the settlement, but merely supplemented the American and English population.

From January 19 to July 5, 1779, sixty-three Spanish families totaling two hundred and three souls reached "Galveztown," but disease wiped out a good number of them, or else they abandoned the shores of the Amite river. What remained of the Spanish at "Galveztown" was but a miserable few. One can only conclude that the "islenos" could not adjust themselves to the surrounding and educated population, and they woefully lacked the initiative to make the attempt. Hence, the settlement at "Galveztown" ended in failure for the Canary Islanders.

Nueva Iberia

On January 15, 1779, Don Bernardo de Galvez, the Spanish Governor of Louisiana, mentions in a despatch, the arrival of families from Malaga, Spain. Most of these recruits settled in the Attakapas country of Louisiana at a place called "Nueva Iberia." Here, they were under the Captain-Commandant; Don Francisco Bouligny. They cultivated at first flax and hemp, but without success. Soon, they were raising cattle on the vast prairies of the Attakapas. There were at least 500 people involved in the migration, but all were not from Malaga. A few scattered Canary Islanders joined their Spanish-speaking fellow nationals of "Nueva Iberia". The vanguard of Acadian exiles had previously been conducted to the land of Evangeline by the Militia Captain Louis Antoine Andry as early as 1765. But by 1778 and later, the Acadians arrived from different points of the compass. This new influx added to the natural complexities of the Spanish administration in Louisiana.

San Bernardo de Galvez

The most important settlement of the "islenos" in Louisiana was that of "San Bernardo de Galvez." The Spaniards called the district, "Terra de Buyes", known by the French as the "Terre-aux-boeuf," the land of the oxen, largely due to the great number of oxen that was once found there.

The colony was founded a few miles miles below New Orleans at a place called "San Bernardo de Galvez" which the settler named in honor of the patron saint of Governor Galvez. The site chosen was a fertile and high strip of land lying between the Mississippi river on the West, and a bayou to the East.

Either before or shortly after the arrival of the Canary Islanders, Pierre Philippe Enguerrand de Marigny de Mandeville, an infantry officer in Louisiana, owned considerable lands in the Saint Bernard area. He was duly appointed by Governor Galvez, the Captain-Commandant of the "islenos." Due to his considerable wealth, he donated various concessions to the Canary Islanders when they arrived in the parish of Saint Bernard. At his death, the vast land holdings in New Orleans and the adjacent areas went to his son, the famous Bernard Xavier de Marigny de Mandeville.

The next Captain-Commandant of the "islenos" was the distinguished militia officer, Pierre Denis de Laronde. At the death of his widow, her succession noted that on April 1, 1788, Pierre Philippe de Marigny de Mandeville ceded an island formed by the "Terre-aux-boeuf", Lake Lery, and Dog River, to Pierre Denis de Laronde, and that it had been duly surveyed by the Royal Engineer, Don Carlos Laveau Trudeau.

The land on which the village of "Delacroix" is built once belonged to the noble Dusuau Delacroix family of Louisiana, and consequently, the primitive-looking fishing village was named in honor of the family. In 1891, the priest of the Parish of Saint Bernard, Reverend Douatre, visited the widow of the Count Dusuau Delacroix in Paris. She gave to Father Douatre the clear title to six acres of land, and added two religious statues for good measure. This land is found opposite the quaint but picturesque cemetery by the banks of the "Terre-aux-boeuf."

"Terra de Buyes" was noted at one time for her vast sugarlands and fine antebellum plantations. Here, the great Confederate General, Pierre Gustave Toutant Beauregard was born. And here too, was "Sevastopol", "Kenilworth," "Contreras," and other major sugar plantations. Meanwhile, the old bayou of the "Terre-aux-boeuf" flowed serenely to Lake Lery and Lake Borgne. Reggio, Beauregard, Olivier de Vezin, Jorda, Marin y Argote and Proctor, were but a few of the familial names of the affluent and wealthy planters of the district.

Unlike other Spanish settlements in Louisiana, the "islenos" of the "Terre-aux-boeuf" earned a good living catching fish and fur-bearing animals, and during the slack season they found work on the various sugar estates. Then too, they were in close proximity to New Orleans, where they could invariably trade and secure a fair profit for their produce.

The Canary Islanders seemingly lived without care. They were a devout and yet superstitious people. The writer recalls that many years ago he saw them affix large religious pictures to their modest doorways, this to dispel the fury of the annual hurricanes and high tides. In this land of vast marsh prairies they found stoicism and humor where they lived and married as a sheltered clan among themselves. Their means of conveyance to and from New Orleans was the sturdy farm cart and the ponderous oxen. In the twilight, wealthy planters could see and hear these carts as they followed one another on the muddy banks of the "Terre-aux-boeuf," with their occupants gaily jesting and laughing as they slowly made their way on the roads near the Mississippi, and up to the French Market at New Orleans. The gaily dressed senoritas joined the caravan for the pleasure of shopping in the Creole city. Always the command of their elders was obeyed. But one can truly say that desires went no further than their beloved fishing settlement to which they had brought their folklore and chansonnettes. To conclude, one might say that here at "San Bernardo de Galvez", the volunteer recruits of a historical migration found a halcyon cove of contentment.

The treasured microfilms of the Spanish Government on the Canary Island Migration to Louisiana provide a stimulating incentive in my endless quest to reveal the romance and grandeur of the great Spanish Domination of Louisiana.

I am indebted to the Government of Spain and the Archives of Seville and to Senor Maria Teresa Garcia, its most gracious librarian for their kind assistance.

To my dear wife Audrey who patiently offered constructive criticism and inspiration, along with the onerous task of indexing the passenger listings of the eight ships, I offer my sincere thanks.

New Orleans,
March 1970

Sidney Louis Villeré

Contents

	Page
Introduction	iii
Maps	xiii
SS Sacremento	1
San Ignacio de Loyola	12
La Victoria	29
San Juan Nepomuceno	41
La Santa Fas	50
El Sagrado Corazon de Jesus	67
Terra de Buyes	81
Fragata Llamada Margarita	88
SS Trinadad	90

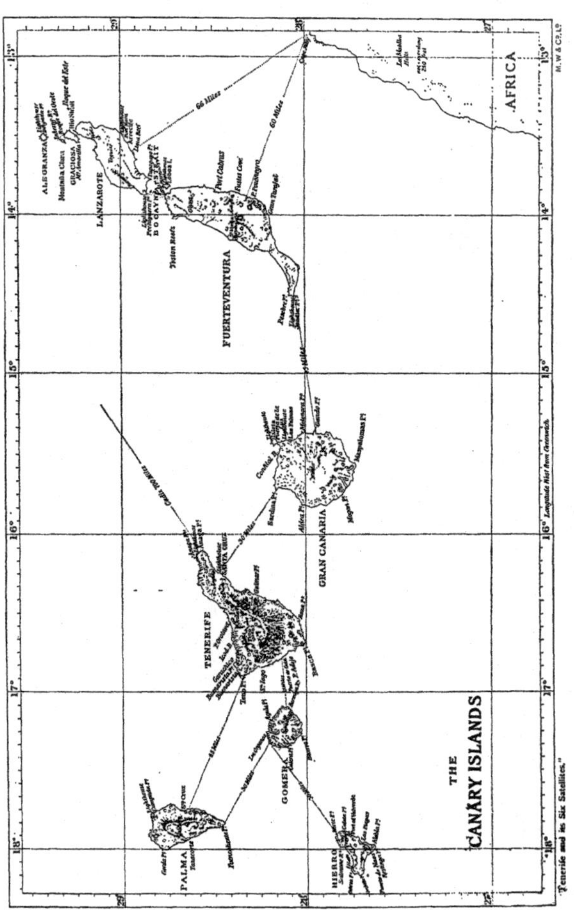
THE
CANARY ISLANDS
AFRICA
LANZAROTE
FUERTEVENTURA
GRAN CANARIA
TENERIFE
GOMERA
PALMA
HIERRO
"Tenerife and its Six Satellites."

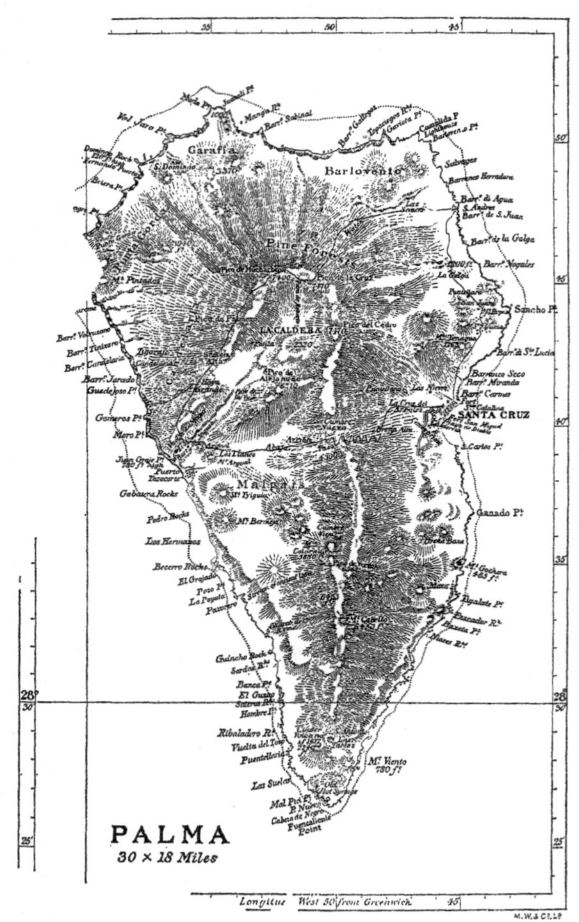
PALMA
30 × 18 Miles
Garafia
Barlovento
Pine Forests
LA CALDERA
SANTA CRUZ
Malpais
Sancho Pt.
Ganado Pt.
Longitue West 50 from Greenwich

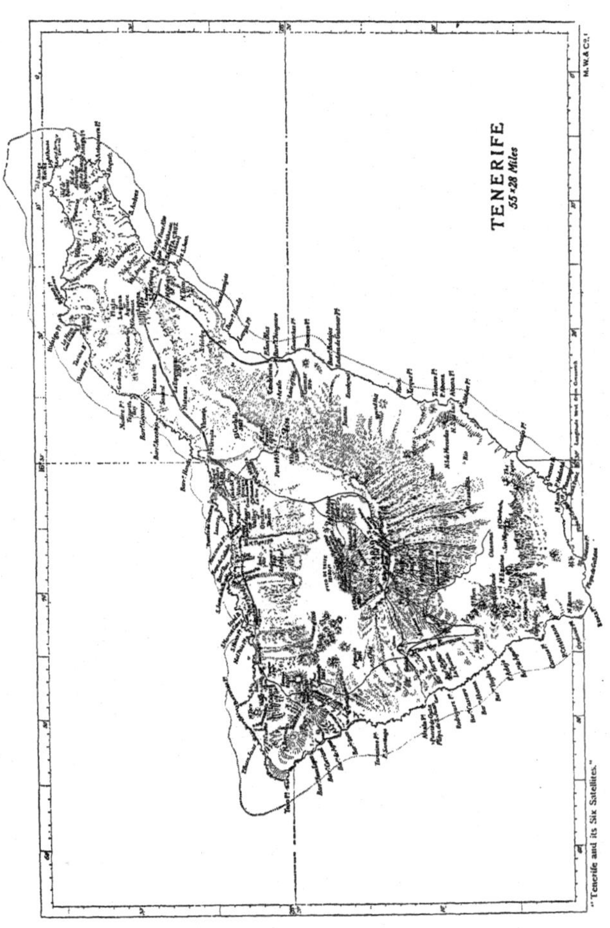

"Tenerife and its Six Satellites."

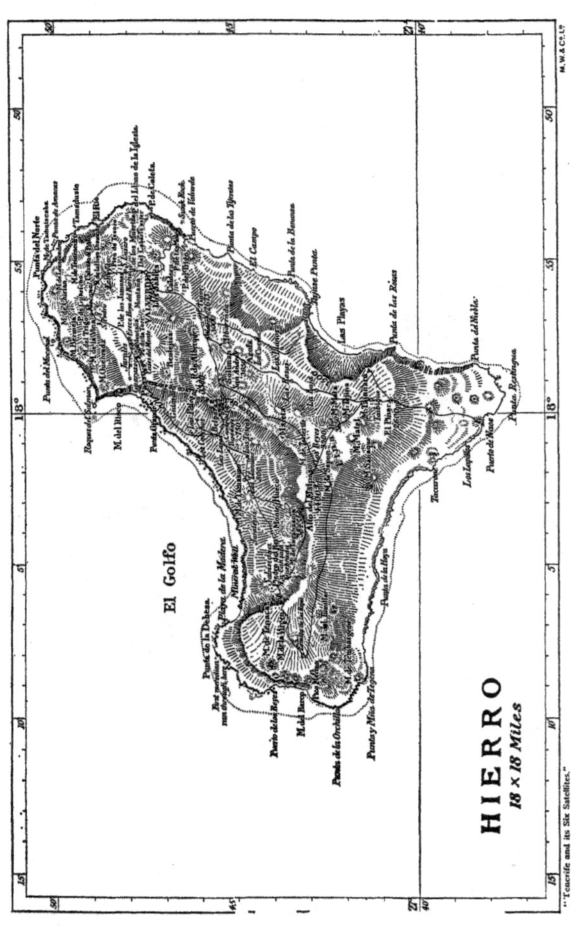
El Golfo
HIERRO
18 × 18 Miles
"Tenerife and its Six Satellites."
M. W. & Co. Ld

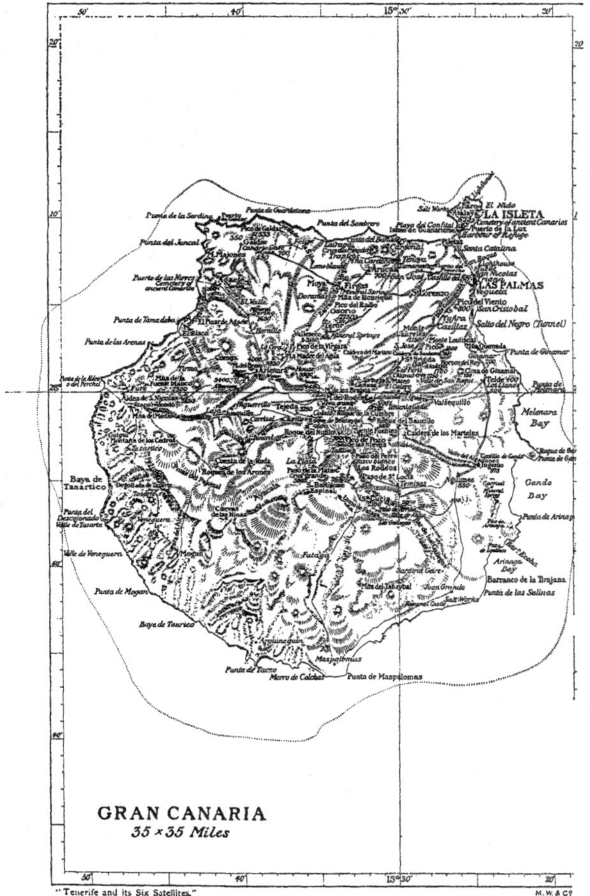

" Tenerife and its Six Satellites."

M. W. & Co.

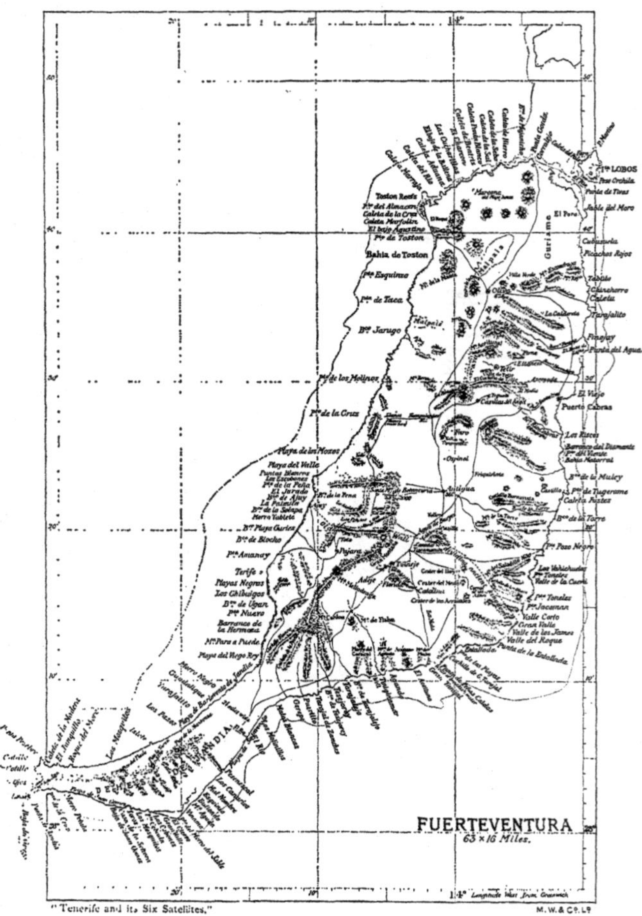
FUERTEVENTURA
63 × 16 Miles.
Iᵃ LOBOS
Toston Reefs
Pᵗᵃ de Toston
Bahia de Toston
Pᵗᵃ Esquinzo
Pᵗᵃ de Taca
Bᵒ Jarugo
Pᵗᵃ de los Molinos
Pᵗᵃ de la Cruz
Playa de los Mozes
Playa del Valle
Bᵒ Playa Gariza
Pᵗᵃ Amanay
Terife
Playas Negras
Puerto Cabras
El Viejo
Las Rises
Pᵗᵃ Poso Negro
Valle Corto
Gran Valle
Valle del Roque
Punta de la Entallada
Antigua
Pajara
Tuineje
Malpaiz
Guriame
El Poro
Cubasnola
Picachos Rojos
Tabiche
Fingjay
Punta del Agua
Longitude West from Greenwich
"Tenerife and its Six Satellites."
M.W.&Cº Lᵈ

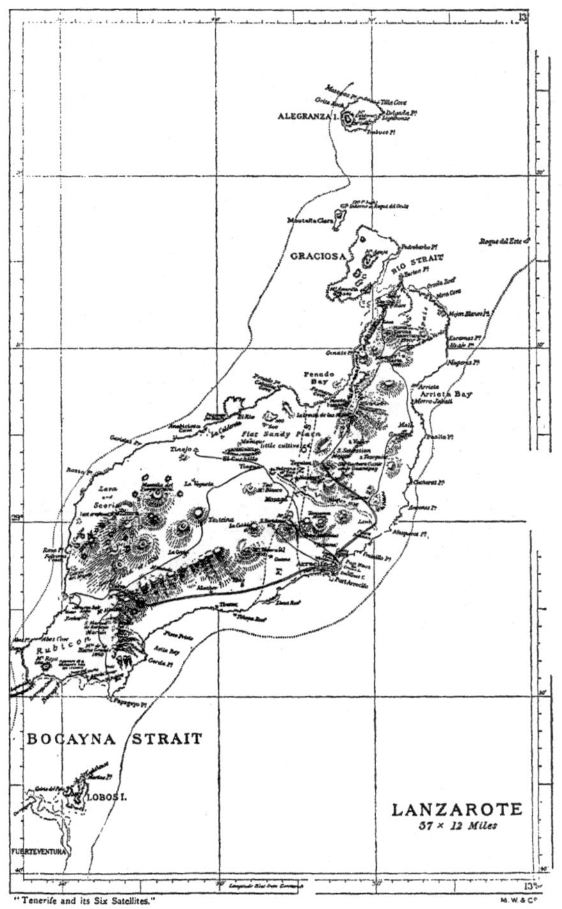

"Tenerife and its Six Satellites." M. W. & Co.

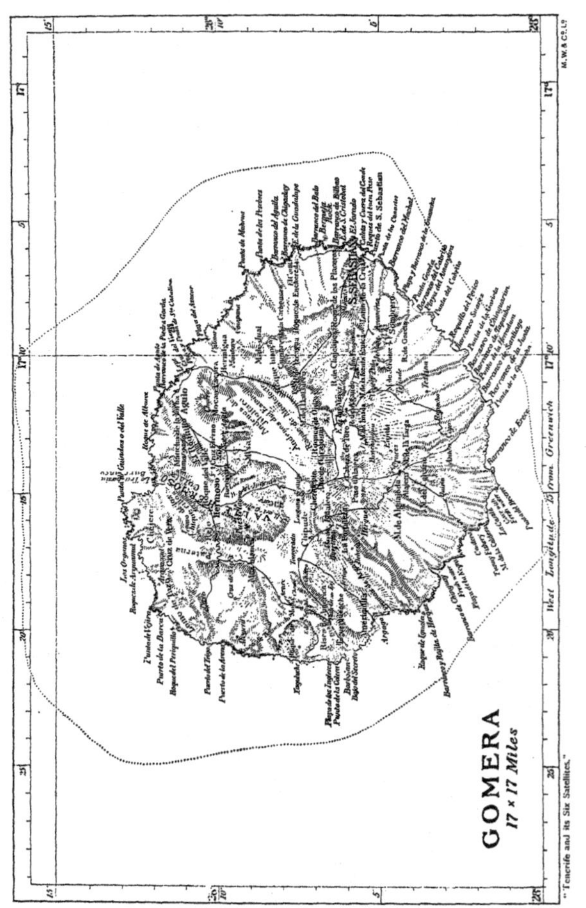
GOMERA
17 × 17 Miles
West Longitude from Greenwich
"Tenerife and its Six Satellites."

RECRUITS AND THEIR FAMILIES

WHO EMBARKED ON

JULY 26, 1778

ON BOARD THE

"SS SACREMENTO"

UNDER THE COMMAND OF

CAPTAIN BENITO RIPOLLI y BARCELO

JULY 26, 1778.

INFANTRY REGIMENT OF LOUISIANA

Relative to the recruits in garrison who were married or single, destined for Havana so as to embark on the "SS SACREMENTO", with the Louisiana Battalion under the command of Captain Benito Ripolli y Barcelo as of this date.

	Armed Personnel		Persons	Total
1.	VENTURA PERDAMO y QUINTANA			
	wife-	MARIA HERNANDEZ	2	3
	dau.	MARIA PERDAMO y QUINTANA, 8 mo.		
1.	DOMINGO GRILLO		1	1
1.	DOMINGO ANTONIO de ACOSTA			
	wife-	FRANCESCA MAURICIO	2	2
1.	DOMINGO GARCIA		1	1
1.	SEVASTIAN GARCIA		1	1
1.	BLAS DIAZ de ENEDA		1	1
1.	ANTONIO GARCIA		1	1
	Wife:	ANA GONZALES		
	Son-	AMARO GARCIA, age 16 years		
	Son-	LAZARO GARCIA " 14 "	4	6
	Son-	FELIX GARCIA " 5-1/2		
	Dau-	MARIA GARCIA " 3 "		
1.	FRANCISCO AMADO		1	1
1.	TOMAS de SILVA		1	1
1.	JOSEF GONZALES		2	2
	Wife:	MARIA CANDELARIA		
1.	JOSEF ANTONIO de la CRUZ		2	2
	Wife:	JOSEFA MARTIN		
1.	JUAN RODRIGUEZ SUAREZ		3	3
	Wife:	MARIA de la CONCEPCION DOMINGUEZ		
	Dau-	MARIA SUAREZ, age 15 years		
1.	DOMINGO HERNANDEZ			
	Wife:	ANDREA JOSEFA de la CRUZ	4	6
	Son-	VICENTE HERNANDEZ, age 15 years		
	Son-	CLEMENTO HERNANDEZ " 5 "		
	Son-	ANTONIO HERNANDEZ " 16 "		
	Son-	GERONIMO HERNANDEZ " 4 "		
			27	33

	Armed Personnel	Persons	Total
1.	JOSEF QUINTERO Wife: ANTONIA de ARMAS Son- ANTONIO QUINTERO, age 10 years Dau- ANTONIA QUINTERO, " 8 "	3	4
1.	VENTURO GERONIMO GUIZOLA	1	1
1.	JUAN JOSEF de HERRERA, Widower Son- PEDRO de HERRERA, age 10 years Son- AUGUSTIN de HERRERA, age 5 years	2	3
1.	NICOLAS HERNANDEZ Wife: CATALINA LIAS	2	2
1.	PEDRO TORRALVA	1	1
1.	FRANCISCO GONZALES	1	1
1.	DOMINGO DIAZ Wife: MARIA ALONSO Son- SLAVADOR DIAZ	3	3
1.	JOACHIM de PAEZ	1	1
1.	JOSEF ANTONIO GONZALEZ Wife: MARIA PEREZ	2	2
1.	BERNARDO PEDRES	1	1
1.	ALEXANDRO de los SANTOS Wife: BERNARDA GARCIA Dau- MARIA de los SANTOS, age 4 years Son- DOMINGO de los SANTOS, age 2 years	2	4
1.	JOSEF ANTONIO DIAZ Wife: BLASINI TORRARDO	2	2
1.	MANUEL NUNEZ VILLAVICENCIO Wife: JOSEFA SUAREZ Dau- MARIA del CARMEN NUNEZ, age 12 years Dau- MARIA NUNEZ VILLAVICENCIO, age 4 yrs Son- ESTEVAN NUNEZ " , " 7 " Son- IGNACIO NUNEZ " , " 2 " Son- JOSEFA NUNEZ " , " 2 "	7	7
1.	JOSEF MARTIN, 2nd. Wife: RITA de LEON Dau- MARIA MARTIN, age 5 years Son- DOMINGO MARTIN " 2 "	2	4
1.	FRANCISCO GONZALES TOLEDO Wife: BERNARDA HERNANDEZ Dau- MARIA TOLEDO, age 5 years	2	3

	Armed Personnel	Persons	Total
1.	JOSEF MARTIN	2	2
	Wife: MARIA ST. CHRISTO LEON		
1.	JUAN MEDERON		
	Wife: JOSEFA MARTINEZ DUENDE	2	3
	Dau- FRANCESCA MEDERON, age 5 years		
1.	ANTONIO de los REYES	1	1
1.	AUGUSTIN PINTO de LEON		
	Wife: MARIA CASANAS		
	Son- JUAN de LEON, age 13 years		
	Dau- BERNARDA de LEON, age 11 years	4	6
	Dau- MARIA de LEON, age 7 years		
	Dau- MARTELA de LEON, age 5 years		
1.	JOSEFAAUGUSTIN		
	Wife: ISABEL GARCIA	2	3
	Son- PABLO AUGUSTIN		
1.	ANTONIO SILVA	2	2
	Wife: CLARA POSCAS de ARVELO		
1.	JOSEF HERNANDEZ MONTESINO		
	Wife: POLONIO RODRIGUEZ CORREA	3	3
	Dau- MARIA JOSEFA HERNANDEZ MONTESINO		
1.	DOMINGO GARCIA	2	3
	Wife: AMBROSEA MONTESINO		
	Son- JUAN GARCIA, age 4 years		
1.	JOSEF ANTONIO SILVERIO		
	Wife: MARIA PEREZ	3	7
	Son- JULIAN SIVERIO, age 16 years		
	Son- PASCUAL SIVERIO, age 4 years		
	Son- JOSEF SIVERIO, age 7 years		
	Dau- MARIA SIVERIO, age 5 years		
	Dau- ROSALIA SIVERIA, age 2 years		
1.	BALTASAR MARTIN		
	Wife: ROSALIA PEREZ		
	Son- ANTONIO MARTIN, age 18 years	4	7
	Son- ANDRES MARTIN, age 9 years		
	Dau- MARIA MARTIN, age 10 years		
	Son- LEANDRO MARTIN, age 8 years		
	Son- JUAN MARTIN, age 4 years		
1.	JUAN NERIS	1	1
1.	DON DIEGO LACHHART		
	Wife: DONA MARIA AUGUSTIN ESTEVES		
	Dau- JUANA LACHHART, age 5 years		
	Dau- BARBARA LACHHART, age 11 years		
	Dau- MARIA LACHHART, age 4 years		

	Armed Personnel	Persons	Total
1.	JUAN GONZALES	1	1
1.	JOSEF HERNANDEZ LOPEZ Wife: MARIA del CARMEN Dau- MARIA HERNANDEZ LOPEZ age 18 Dau- MARIA HERNANDEZ LOPEZ, age 15 Dau- JOSEFA HERNANDEZ LOPEZ, age 13	5	5
1.	BLAS ANTONIO MONTESINO Wife: AUGUSTINA GARCIA MARTEL	2	2
1.	JUAN FRANCISCO GUTTERREZ	1	1
1.	ANDRES PADRINO Wife: INES MARIA	2	2
1.	JOSEF MARTIN Wife: MICAELA GARCIA	2	2
1.	ANTONIO JOSEF RODRIGUEZ	1	1
1.	CHRISTOVAL ANTONIO GOMEZ	1	1
1.	MANUEL MATHEOS	1	1
1.	MATHIA GONZALES	1	1
1.	MARCOS FRANCISCO LABRADOR Wife: FRANCESCA ANDREA ABREU Son- ANTONIO FRANCISCO LABRADOR, 17 years Dau- ANTONIA LABRADOR, age 22 years Dau- JOSEFA LABRADOR, age 19 years Dau- MARIA LABRADOR, age 5 years Son- JOSEF LABRADOR, age 11 years Dau- BARBARA LABRADOR, age 3 years	6	8
1.	JUAN GONZALES CARBO Wife: ANDREA RUIZ Dau- CECELIA CARBO, age 25 years Dau- LORENZA CARBA, age 24 years Dau- MARIA CARBO, age 17 years Dau- RITA CARBO, age 15 years Dau- ANDREA CARBO, age 13 years Son- JOSEF CARBO, age 9 years Son- AUGUSTIN CARBO, age 8 years Son- DOMINGO CARBO, age 3 years Dau- JUANA CARBO, age 11 months	8	11
1.	JULIAN GODOY	1	1
1.	JUAN COBRA	1	1

Armed Personnel	Persons	Total
1. ANDRES DOMINGUEZ, Widower Dau- MARIA DOMINGUEZ, age 14 years Son- JUAN DOMINGUEZ, age 12 years Dau- PETRA DOMINGUEZ, age 11 years Dau- BARBARA DOMUNGUEZ, age 2 years	4	5
1. JOSEF MIRANDA	1	1
1. JOSEF RODRIGUEZ Wife: MARIA AUGUSTINA de GUERRA Son- DOMINGO RODRIGUEZ, age 14 years Son- FRANCISCO RODRIGUEZ, age 10 years	4	4
1. FRANCISCO CASTANEDO Wife: FELIPA PADRON	2	2
	128	166
1. VICENTE ANTONIO NAVARRO	1	1
1. PEDRO MARTIN Wife: MARIA GARCIA Mother: MARIA DORTA	3	3
1. NICOLAS RODRIGUEZ	1	1
1. PEDRO SANTANA	1	1
1. JUAN DIAZ	1	1
1. FRANCISCO BERLOY	1	1
1. JOSEF MARTIN CABRERO	1	1
1. MATHEO MENDEZ	1	1
1. JUAN FRANCISCO PEREZ BLANCO	1	1
1. GUIDO HERNANDEZ Wife: BARBARA GONZALES	2	2
1. PATRICIO JOSEF GARCIA	1	1
1. FRANCISCO XAVIER TRUXILLO Wife: MANUELA ANTONIA MARTELA Son- GREGORIO TRUXILLO, age 17 years Son- JUAN TRUXILLO, age 6 years Son- CHRISTOVAL TRUXILLO, age 5 years Dau- MARIA TRUXILLA, age 18 months.	3	6
1. DIEGO TANES	1	1
1. JOSEF GARCIA	1	1

ARMED PERSONNEL	PERSONS	TOTAL
1. MATHEO GONZALES TAXARDO Wife: LORENZA de ACEVEDO de TEBES Dau- MARIA GONZALES TAXARDO, age 3 years Son- JOSEF GONZALES TAXARDO, age 7 months	2	4
1. ANTONIO QUESADA Wife: MELCHORA CABRAL Son- JOSEF QUESADA, age 12 years Dau- MARIA QUESADA, age 6 years	3	4
1. JOSEF PABLO de LEON	1	1
1. LORENZO LOPEZ	1	1
1. FRANCISCO ANTONIO MALLORQUIN	1	1
1. AMARO GARCIA	1	1
1. FRAMCISCO LELIAN	1	1
1. SILVESTRE de LEON Wife: MARIA DIONISEA de los NIEVES	2	2
1. LUIS ANTONIO de BARGAS	1	1
1. GREGORIO GONZALES Wife: MARIA de la ENCARNACION	2	2
	163	207
1. FRANCISCO MIRANDA	1	1
1. ANTONIO ALONSO	1	1
1. JOSEF CABO	1	1
1. LORENZO HERNANDEZ NEDA	1	1
1. PABLO RODRIGUEZ SIERRA	1	1
1. JOSEF ESCOBAR	1	1
1. FRANCISCO GARCIA	1	1
1. BLAIS GARCIA de ABREO	1	1
1. DIEGO ANTONIO ROMAN Wife: ANTONIA RODRIGUEZ	2	2
1. JOSEF GARCIA GRILLO	1	1
1. NICOLAS PEREZ de ABREO	1	1

	ARMED PERSONNEL	PERSONS	TOTAL
1.	IGNACIO PEREZ ROQUE	1	1
1.	JUAN CANDELARIA GRILLO	1	1
1.	JUAN ANTONIO PRIETO	1	1
1.	ANTONIO AUGUSTIN HERNANDEZ	1	1
1.	CHRISTOVAL SIMON	1	1
1.	ANTONIO JOSEF CARRILLO	1	1
1.	ANTONIO del CASTILLO	1	1
1.	ANTONIO GONZALES GOMEZ	1	1
1.	DOMINGO HERNANDEZ TRUXILLO	1	1
1.	ANTONIO MONTESINO DEMENTE Wife: MARIA ESTEVES Son- LORENZO MONTESINO DEMENTE, age 11 mo.	2	3
1.	ANTONIO JOSEF MORALES Wife: ISABEL MARIA de CANDELARIA Dau- SEVESTIANA MORALES, age 3 years Dau- MARIA MORALES, age 2 years	2	4
1.	MANUEL DIAZ	1	1
1.	JOSEF PLACENSAS	1	1
1.	PEDRO MARTIN	1	1
1.	JOSEF FRANCISCO LOSO	1	1
1.	PEDRO HERRERA	1	1
1.	JOSEF MARTEL	1	1
1.	LUIS BETANCOURT	1	1
1.	JOSEF LOPEZ	1	1
1.	SILVESTRE del RIVERO	1	1
1.	JUAN BENITEZ	1	1
1.	ANDRES DIAZ	1	1
1.	FRANCISCO PEREZ	1	1
1.	FRANCISCO HERNANDEZ Wife: MARIA CHERINE	2	2
		202	249

INDEX
"S.S. SACREMENTO"

ABREO, Blais Garcia de, 6
ABREO, Nicolas Perez de, 6
ABREU, Grancesca Andrea, 4
ACOSTA, Domingo Antonia, 1
ALONSO, Antonio, 6
ALONSO, Maria, 2
AMADO, Framcisco, 1
ARVELO, Clara Poscas de, 3
AUGUSTIN, Josef, 3
AUGUSTIN, Pablo, 3
BARGAS, Luis Antonio de, 6
BENITEZ, Juan, 7
BERLOY, Framcisco, 5
BLANCO, Juan Francisco Perez, 5
CABO, Josef, 6
CABRAL, Melchora, 6
CABRERO, Josef Martin, 5
CANDELARIA, Ysabel Maria de, 7
CANDELARIA, Maria, 1
CARBO, Andrea, 4
CARBO, Augustin, 4
CARBO, Cecelia, 4
CARBO, Domingo, 4
CARBO, Juan Gonzales, 4
CARBO, Juana, 4
CARBO, Lorenza, 4
CARBO, Maria, 4
CARBO, Rita, 4
CARRILLO, Antonio Josef, 7
CASANAS, Maria, 7
CASTANEDO, Framcisco, 5
CHERINE, Maria, 7
CORREA, Polonia Rodriguez, 3
CRUZ, Andrea, Josefa de la, 1
CRUZ, Josef Antonio de la, 1
DEMENTE, Antonio Montesino, 7
DEMENTE, Lorenzo Montesino, 7
DIAZ, Andres, 1
DIAZ, Domingo, 2
DIAZ, Josef Antonio, 2
DIAZ, Manuel, 7
DIAZ, Salvador, 2
DOMINGUEZ, Andres, 5
DOMINGUEZ, Barbara, 5
DOMINGUEZ, Juan, 5
DOMINGUEZ, Maria, 5
DOMINGUEZ, Petra, 5
DORTA, Maria, 5
DUENDE, Josefa Martinez, 3
ENEDA, Blas Diaz de, 1
ESCOBAR, Josef, 6
ESTEVES, Dona Maria Augustin, 3
ESTEVES, Maria, 7
GARCIA, Amaro, 1, 6
GARCIA, Antonio, 1
GARCIA, Domingo, 1, 3
GARCIA, Felix, 1
GARCIA, Framcisco, 6
GARCIA, Josef, 5
GARCIA, Juan, 3
GARCIA, Lazaro, 1
GARCIA, Maria, 1, 5
GARCIA, Micaela, 4
GARCIA, Patricio Josef, 5
GARCIA, Ysabel, 3
GODOY, Julian, 4
GOMEZ, Christoval Antonio, 4
GONZALES, Barbara, 5
GONZALES, Gregoria, 6
GONZALES, Josef Antonio, 2
GONZALES, Juan, 4
GONZALES, Mathia, 4
GRILLO, Domingo, 1
GRILLO, Josef Garcia, 6
GRILLO, Juan Candelario, 7
GUERRA, Maria Augustina de, 5
GUIZOLA, Ventura Geronimo, 2
GUTTERREZ, Juan Francisco, 4
HERNANDEZ, Antonio, 1
HERNANDEZ, Antonio Augustin, 7
HERNANDEZ, Clemento, 1
HERNANDEZ, Domingo, 1
HERNANDEZ, Geronimo, 1
HERNANDEZ, Guido, 5
HERNANDEZ, Vicente, 1
HERRERA, Augustin de, 2
HERRERA, Juan Josef de, 2
HERRERA, Pedro de, 1, 2
LEON, Aigustin Pinto de, 3
LEON, Maria St. Christo, 3
LEON, Rita de, 2
LABRADOR, Antonia, 4
LABRADOR, Antonia, 4
LABRADOR, Barbara, 4
LABRADOR, Josef, 4
LABRADOR, Josefa, 4
LABRADOR, Francisco, 4

INDEX

"S.S. SACREMENTO"

LABRADOR, Maria, 4
LACHHART, Barbara, 3
LACHHART, Don Diego, 3
LACHHART, Juan, 3
LACHHART, Maria, 3
LELIAN, Francisco, 6
LIAS, Catalina, 2
LEON, Rita de, 2
LEON, Maria St. Christo, 3
LEON, Augustin Pinto de, 3
LOPEZ, Josef, 7
LOPEZ, Josefa, 4
LOPEZ, Josef Hernandez, 4
LOPEZ, Lorenzo, 6
LOPEZ, Maria, 4

MALLORQUIN, Francisco Antonio, 6
MARTEL, Augustina Garcia, 4
MARTEL, Josef, 7
MARTELA, Manuela Antonia, 5
MARTIN, Andres, 3
MARTIN, Antonio, 3
MARTIN, Baltasar, 3
MARTIN, Josef, 2, 3,
MARTIN, Josefa, 1
MARTIN, Juan, 1
MARTIN, Leandro, 3
MARTIN, Maria, 2, 3
MARTIN, Pedro, 7
MARTEL, Josef, 7
MARTELA, Manuela Antonia, 5
MATHEOS, Manuel, 5
MIRANDA, Francisco, 6
MIRANDA, Josef, 5
MONTESINO, Smbrosia, 3
MONTESINO, Blas Antonio, 4
MONTESINO, Josef Hernandez, 3
MORALES, Antonio Josef, 7
MORALES, Maria, 7
MORALES, Sevastiana, 7

NAVARRO, Vicente Antonio, 5
NEDA, Lorenza Hernandez, 6
NIEVES, Maria Dionisea de los, 6

PADRINO, Andres, 4
PAEZ, Joaquim de, 2
PEDRES, Bernardo, 2
PEREZ, Framcisco, 7
PEREZ, Maria, 2, 3
PEREZ, Rosalia, 3
PLACENCIA, Josef, 7
PRIETO, Juan Antonio, 7

QUESADA, Antonio, 6
QUESADA, Josef, 6
QUESADA, Maria, 6
QUINTANA, Ventura Perdomo, 1
QUINTANA, Maria Perdomo, 1
QUINTERO, Antonio, 2
QUINTERO, Antonia, 2
QUINTERO, Josef, 2

REYES, Antonio de los, 3
RIVERO, Silvestre del, 7
RODRIGUEZ, Antonia, 6
RODRIGUEZ, Domingo, 5
RODRIGUEZ, Josef, 5
RODRIGUEZ, Francisco, 5
RODRIGUEZ, Nicolas, 5
ROMAN, Diego Antonio, 6
ROQUE, Ignacio Perez, 7

SANTANA, Pedro, 5
SANTOS, Alexandro de los, 3
SANTOS, Domingo de los, 2
SANTOS, Maria de los, 2
SIERRA, Pablo Rodriguez, 6
SILVA, Antonio, 3
SILVA, Tomas de, 1
SIMON, Christoval, 7
SIVERIO, Josef, 3
SIVERIO, Josef Antonio, 3
SIVERIO, Julian, 3
SIVERIO, Maria, 3
SIVERIO, Pasqual, 3
SIVERIO, Rosalia, 3
SUAREZ, Juan Rodriguez, 1
SUAREZ, Maria, 1.

TANES, Diego, 5
TAXARDO, Josef Gonzales, 6
TAXARDO, Maria Gonzales, 6
TAXARDO, Matheo Gonzales, 2
TEBES, Lorenza de Aceveda, 6
TOLEDO, Francisco Gonzales, 2
TOLEDO, Maria, 2
TORRALVA, Pedro, 2
TORRARDO, Blasina, 2
TRUXILLO, Francisco Xavier, 5

INDEX

"S.S. SACREMENTO"

TRUXILLO, Gregoria, 5
TRUXILLO, Juan, 5

VILLAVICENCIO, Manuel Nunez, 2
VILLAVICENCIO, Maria del Carmen Nunez, 2
VILLAVICENCIO, Maria Nunez, 2
VILLAVICENCIO, Estevan Nunez, 2
VILLAVICENCIO, Ignacio Nunez, 2
VILLAVICENCIO, Josefa Nunez, 2

RECRUITS AND THEIR FAMILIES

WHO EMBARKED ON

OCTOBER 9, 1778

ON BOARD THE

"SAN IGNACIO de LOYOLA"

UNDER THE COMMAND OF

DON FELIX FRANCISCO de la ORUO

OCTOBER 9, 1778

INFANTRY REGIMENT OF LOUISIANA

Relatives to the recruits in garrison who were married or single, destined for Havana so as to embark on October 9, 1778 for the Port of New Orleans on the Spanish Frigate named "SAN IGNACIO de LOYOLA". Capitan DON FELIX FRANCISCO de la ORUO.

	Armed Personnel		Total
1.	DON MARTIN FERRY PALAO		
	Wife: DONA ANTONIA PRAST		5
	Dau- DONA OLAYA PALAO	age 17 years	
	Son- DON PEDRO PALAO	" 6 "	
	Dau- DONA MARIA PALAO	" 3 "	
1.	DON IGNACIO FERRY PALAO		1
1.	DON MARTIN FERRY PALAO		1
1.	JUAN HERNANDEZ PESTANO		
	Wife: JUANITA de LEON		2
1.	JUAN ANTONIO ALFONSO		
	Wife: MARIA MARRERO		3
	Son- LUIS ALFONSO	age 2 years	
1.	PABLO ESTEVES		
	Wife: MARIA RODRIGUEZ		2
1.	ANTONIO SUERIO PIMENTEL		
	Wife: MARIA TORRE		7
	Son- MARCIAL PIMENTEL	age 15 years	
	Dau- FRANCESCA PIMENTEL	" 10 "	
	Dau- ISABEL PIMENTEL	" 7 "	
	Step-daughter- ANA MARIA SUARES		
	Step-son BARTHOLOME SUARES		
1.	ANTONIO ESMERALDO		
	Wife: ANGELA GUERRA		3
	Dau- MARIA ESMERALDO,	age 2 years	
1.	JOSEF ANTONIO ALONSO		
	Wife: MANUELA DELGADO		2
1.	FRANCISCO MANUEL GOMEZ		
	Wife: MARIA PERERA		3
	Son- JUAN GOMEZ	age 6 months	

	Armed Personnel			Total
1.	ALONSO RUANO			
	Wife:	IGNACIA CASANAS		5
	Son-	JOSEF RUANO	age 7 years	
	Dau-	MARIA RUANO	" 2 "	
	Sister-	ISABEL RUANO		
1.	MATHIAS HERNANDEZ NEDA			
	Wife:	JOSEFA CASALTA		5
	Son-	JOSEF NEDA	" 6 "	
	Son-	DOMINGO NEDA	" 4 "	
	Dau-	MARIA NEDA	" 11 months	
1.	ANTONIO GARCIA de ABREU			
	Wife:	AUGUSTINA SANCHEZ		3
	Dau-	RAFAELA GARCIA	" 18 years	
1.	ANTONIO SUARES			
	Wife:	JUANA SUARES		3
	Son-	FRANCISCO SUARES	" 10 months	
1.	GULLERMO GONZALES CHOCHO			
	Wife:	MARIA GIL		3
	Son-	SEVASTIEN GONZALES CHOCHO	" 3 months	
1.	JOSEF RODRIGUEZ CHARNERO			
	Wife:	MARIA GARCIA		4
	Son-	DOMINGO CHARNERO	" 2 years	
	Son-	PEDRO CHARNERO	" 7 months	
1.	PABLO RUIZ			
	Wife:	MARIA OLIVARES		3
	Son-	JUAN RUIZ	" 4 years	
1.	FELIPE ANTILES			
	Wife:	JUANA XIMENEZ		6
	Son-	JUAN ANTILES	" 11 "	
	Son-	ANTONIO ANTILES	" 7 "	
	Dau-	MARIA ANTILES	" 2 "	
	Bro-	JUAN CORJOLA	" 15 "	
1.	JOSEF HIDALGO			
	Wife:	ISABEL SAMBRANA	5 "	
	Son-	GREGORO HIDALGO	" 10 "	
	Dau-	FRANCESCA HIDALGO	" 9 "	5
	Son-	JUAN HIDALGO	" 10 months	
				66
1.	JOSEF ANTONIO RODRIGUEZ			
	Wife:	JUANA de la CRUZ		4
	Dau-	MARIA RODRIGUEZ	" 4 years	
	Dau-	SEVASTIANA RODRIGUEZ	" 3 "	

	Armed Personnel			Total
1.	JOSEF MORALES			
	Wife:	ANTONIA VIERA		5
	Dau-	MARIA MORALES	age 6 years	
	Dau-	CATALINA MORALES	" 4 "	
	Dau-	IGNACIA MORALES	" 10 months	
1.	FRANCISCO ALVARADO MACHADO			1
1.	FRANCISCO SANCHEZ			
	Wife:	MARIA CAVALLERO		4
	Son-	JUAN SANCHEZ	age 2 years	
	Son-	FRANCISCO SANCHEZ	" 1 "	
1.	ANTONIO HERNANDEZ			
	Wife:	SEVASTIANA MONTESDOCA		
	Son-	JUAN HERNANDEZ	" 12 "	5
	Son-	LUIS HERNANDEZ	1 "	
	Dau-	MARIA HERNANDEZ	" 2 "	
1.	ANTONIO SANCHEZ			
	Wife:	JUANA LOPEZ		3
	Dau-	ANDREA SANCHEZ	" 9 months	
1.	JOSEF PERERA SANCHEZ			
	Wife:	MARIA SANTANA		4
	Son-	FRANCISCO SANCHEZ	" 2 years	
	Sister-	ISABEL ANTONIA de CANOS		
1.	JOSEF PERERA			
	Wife:	MARIA RAMIRES		8
	Dau-	MARIA PERERA	age 13 "	
	Dau-	CATALINA PERERA	" 11 "	
	Dau-	JOSEFA PERERA	" 9 "	
	Dau-	FRANCESCA PERERA	" 7	
	Dau-	LUISA PERERA	" 5	
	Dau-	ISABEL PERERA	" 3 months	
1.	JUAN ALEMAN			
	Wife:	JUANA RAMIRES		
	Son-	ANTONIO ALEMAN	" 14 years	7
	Son-	BALTASAR ALEMAN	" 5 "	
	Son-	PEDRO ALEMAN	" 2 "	
	Dau-	JOSEFA ALEMAN	" 9 "	
	Dau-	SEVASTIANA ALEMAN	" 7 "	
1.	JUAN XIMINEZ			
	Dau-	JUANA XIMINEZ	" 20 "	3
	Dau-	MARIA XIMINEZ	" 14 "	
1.	LORENZO HERNANDEZ			
	Wife:	MARIA XIMINEZ		4
	Dau-	ANA HERNANDEZ	" 2 "	
	Dau-	MARIA HERNANDEZ	" 5 months	

	Armed Personnel			Total
1.	BERNARDINO GIMONY			
	Wife:	FRANCESCA ANA POLIER		2
1.	JOSEF ALESANDRO PEREZ			
	Wife:	NICOLOSA CAMBALUZ		3
	Dau-	MARIA PEREZ	age 7 years	
1.	VICENTE DELGADO			
	Wife:	FELIPA XIMINEZ		4
	Dau-	ISABEL DELGADO	" 3 "	
	Dau-	SEVASTIANA DELGADO	" 3 months	
1.	SIMON CASIMIRO			
	Wife:	CATALINA GONZALES		2
1.	MATHIAS MARTIN			
	Wife:	MARIA MAGDALENA		4
	Son-	JUAN MARTIN	age 4 years	
	Dau-	MARIA MARTIN	" 2 "	
1.	BARTOLOME FERNANDEZ			
	Wife:	CATALINA MIRELES	" 4 "	
	Son-	JUAN FERNANDEZ	" 13 "	4
	Son-	VICENTE FERNANDEZ	" 5 "	
1.	DOMINGO VICENTE MORALES			
	Wife:	GREGORIA HIDALGO		2
1.	GASPAR ORTIZ LOPEZ			
	Wife:	MARIA SANCHEZ		4
	Son-	JUAN LOPEZ	" 3 "	
	Dau-	MARIA LOPEZ	" 1 "	
1.	JOSEF BERMUZEZ			3
	Wife:	MARIA RAMIREZ		
	Dau-	CATALINA BERMUDEZ	" 3 months	
1.	CHRISTOVAL FALCON			
	Wife:	JOSEFA MARTIN	"	
	Dau-	ANTONIA FALCON	" 9 months	5
	Dau-	CATALINA FALCON	" 4 years	
	Sister-	ANTONIA MARTIN		
1.	CHRISTOVAL QUINTERO			
	Wife:	MARIA RUANO	" 5 "	
	Son-	CHRISTOVAL QUINTERO	" 18 "	5
	Dau-	MARIA QUINTERO	" 14 "	
	Dau-	BEATRIS QUINTERO	" 10 "	
1.	ANTONIO RAMIRES			
	Wife:	ANA SANTANA		2

	Armed Personnel			Total
1.	GASPAR FALCON			
	Wife:	FRANCESCA MATHEO		
	Son-	JUAN FALCON	age 4 years	4
	Son-	MIGUEL FALCON	2 "	
1.	GREGORIA BERMUDEZ			
	Wife:	ANA NAVARRO		6
	Son-	DIEGO BERMUDEZ	14 "	
	Son-	CLEMENTO BERMUDEZ	4 "	
	Son-	JOSEF BERMUDEZ	6 "	
	Dau-	MARIA BERMUDEZ	16 "	
1.	AUGUSTIN SANCHEZ			
	Wife:	FRANCESCA ORTIZ	age	2
1.	JOSEF ANTONIO VENTURA			
	Wife:	ANTONIA PEREZ		5
	Son-	JOSEF VENTURA	age 2 years	
	Dau-	LORENZA VENTURA	" 7 "	
	Dau-	MARIA VENTURA	" 2 "	
1.	DOMINGO HIEDRA			1
1.	ANTONIO MARTIN			1
1.	ESTEVAN HERNANDEZ			1
1.	GREGORIO JUDAS RANDO			
	Wife:	MELCHORA de los REYES		4
	Son-	JOSEF RANDO	age 3 years	
	Dau-	MARIA RANDO	" 8 "	
1.	JUAN MELIAN			
	Wife:	MARIA ORTIZ		2
1.	ANTONIO de FUENTES			
	Wife:	MARCELA PEREZ		7
	Son-	JUAN de FUENTES	age 11 years	
	Son-	FRANCISCO de FUENTES	" 8 "	
	Son-	PEDRO de FUENTES	" 6 "	
	Son-	JOSEF de FUENTES	" 4 "	
	Dau-	ANA de FUENTES	" 2 "	
				187
1.	LUIS MACIAS			
	Wife:	TOMASA de BORLES		6
	Son-	MIGUEL MACIAS	" 17 "	
	Son-	FRANCISCO MACIAS	" 13 "	
	Son-	JOSEF MACIAS	" 4 "	
	Dau-	FRANCESCA MACIAS	" 3 "	

Armed Personnel

			Total
1.	JUAN SANCHEZ		
Wife:	MARIA FRANCESCA MARTEL		5
Dau-	MARIA SANCHEZ	age 11 years	
Son-	JOSEF SANCHEZ	" 8	
Son-	BARTOLOME SANCHEZ	" 5	
1.	ANTONIO ALONSO		
Wife:	RITA ANDREA		4
Dau-	ANTONIA ALONSO	" 5 "	
Son-	AUGUSTIN ALONSO	" 2 "	
1.	ANTONIO PEREZ GORDILLO		
Wife:	FRANCESCA GONZALES		
Son-	DOMINGO GORDILLO	" 13 "	
Son-	LUCAS GORDILLO	" 10 "	
Son-	ANTONIO GORDILLO	" 5 "	8
Son-	FRANCISCO GORDILLO	" 4 "	
Son-	JOSEF GORDILLO	" 12 "	
Son-	GONZALO GORDILLO	" 2 "	
1.	FELIPE ANTONIO de las MENDES		
Wife:	RUFINA FRANCESCA		3
Dau-	MARIA de las MENDES	" 5 "	
1.	SALVADOR SANCHEZ		
Wife:	AGUEDA DOMINGUEZ		4
Son-	FELIPE SANCHEZ	" 9 months	
Sister-	MARIA RAMIRES		
1.	JOSEF ESPINO		
Wife:	MARIA ACOSTA		3
Son-	FERNANDO ESPINO	" 3 years	
1.	JOSEF JUAN de BARRIOS		
Wife:	BERNARDA NUNEZ		
Dau-	MARIA de BARRIOS	" 4 "	4
Dau-	BARBARA de BARRIOS	" 1 "	
			224
1.	SALVADOR LUIS RAVELO		
Wife:	AUGUSTINA GONZALES		6
Son-	DOMINGO RAVELO	" 18 "	
Son-	JOSEF RAVELO	" 4 "	
Dau-	JOSEFA RAVELO	" 1 "	
Dau-	MARIA RAVELO	" 9 "	
1.	CHRISTOVAL de MESA		
Wife:	JOSEFA GONZALES		3
Son-	JOSEF de MESA	" 1 "	

	Armed Personnel			Total
1.	SALVADOR VIERA			
	Wife:	ANTONIA VIERA		7
	Son-	ANTONIO VIERA	age 8 years	
	Son-	SEVASTIAN VIERA	" 5 "	
	Dau-	MARIA VIERA	" 12 "	
	Dau-	ANDREA VIERA	" 10 "	
	Dau-	MARIA LEONOR VIERA	" 2 "	
1.	LORENZO RODRIGUEZ de LEON			
	Wife:	MARIA ESPINO		5
	Son-	LUIS de LEON	" 12 "	
	Son-	ANTONIO de LEON	" 8 "	
	Dau-	SEVASTIANA de LEON	" 6 "	
1.	JUAN ESPINO			
	Wife:	JOACHINA SOLIER		3
	Sou-	MIGUEL ESPINO	" 1 "	
1.	CHRISTOVAL OJEDA			
	Wife:	JOSEFA FIGUEROA		6
	Son-	CHRISTOVAL OJEDA	" 17 "	
	Son-	ANTONIO OJEDA	8 "	
	Dau-	FRANCESCA OJEDA	" 20 "	
	Dau-	MARIA OJEDA	" 12 "	
1.	MANUEL OJEDA			
	Wife:	FRANCESCA MEDINA		4
	Son-	JUAN OJEDA	" 8 "	
	Dau-	MARIA OJEDA	" 3 "	
1.	JOSEF ANTONIO de la SANTA			2
	Wife:	MARIA BORJE		
1.	GREGORIA OJEDA			
	Wife:	MARIA SUARES		6
	Dau-	MARIA OJEDA	" 5 "	
	Dau-	JOSEFA OJEDA	" 3 "	
	Dau-	ROSALIA OJEDA	" 1 "	
		CATALINA QUINTANA		
1.	JUAN ALVARADO			
	Wife:	MARIA SUARES		5
	Son-	TONAS ALVARADO	" 4 "	
	Dau-	YSABEL ALVARADO	" 2 "	
	Sister-	FRANCESCA ANTONIA ALVARADO		
1.	JOSEF ANGEL QUINTANA			
	Wife:	AUGUSTINA MONZON		
	Dau-	MARIA QUINTANA	" 17 "	
	Dau-	CATALINA QUINTANA	" 15 "	6
	Son-	MANUEL QUINTANA	" 10 "	
	Son-	DIEGO QUINTANA	" 8 "	

Armed Personnel			Total
1.	JOSEF del PINO		
Wife:	RITA MONZON		3
Dau-	MARIA del PINO	age 7 months	
1.	ANTONIO RODRIGUEZ		
Wife:	MARIA JORGE		7
Son-	JUAN RODRIGUEZ	" 7 years	
Son-	JOSEF RODRIGUEZ	" 8 "	
Dau-	MARIA RODRIGUEZ	" 3 "	
Dau-	FRANCESCA RODRIGUEZ	" 2 "	
Son-	FRANCISCO RODRIGUEZ	" 2 months	
1.	DOMINGO CABRERA		
Wife:	RITA SANCHEZ		3
Son-	FELIPE CABRERA	" 5 years	
1.	PEDRO BARRERO		
Wife:	MARIA ANTONIA		3
Dau-	ANTONIA BARRERO	" 4 months	
1.	GABRIEL HERNANDEZ		
Wife:	BARBARA MELIAN	" 4 years	4
Dau-	VICENTE HERNANDEZ	" 17 "	
Son-	FELIX HERNANDEZ	" 15 "	
1.	ANTONIO GUSMAN		
Wife:	FRANCESCA GUERRA		2
			299
1.	DOMINGO ANTONIO ASCANO		
Wife:	MARIA HERNANDEZ		
Son-	PEDRO ASCANO	" 5 "	6
Dau-	JUANA ASCANO	" 7 "	
Dau-	MARIA ASCANO	" 3 "	
Dau-	MICAELA ASCANO	" 6 months	
1.	AUGUSTIN ROMERO		
Wife:	POLONIO RODRIGUEZ		6
Son-	JOSEF ROMERO	" 12 years	
Son-	DOMINGO ROMERO	" 10 "	
Son-	JUAN ROMERO	" 7 "	
Son-	AUGUSTIN ROMERO	" 4 "	
1.	DIEGO RAFAEL de BARRIOS		
Wife:	TERESA CAMACHO		3
Dau-	FRANCESCA de BARRIOS	" 2 months	
1.	BARTOLOME-DIAZ		
Wife:	JOSEFA AGUILAR		
Son-	FERNANDO DIAZ	" 13 years	
Son-	AUGUSTIN DIAZ	" 5 "	
Dau-	FRANCESCA DIAZ	" 7 "	
Dau-	JOSEFA DIAZ	" 4 "	

		Armed Personnel		Total
1.		CHRISTOVAL RODRIGUEZ		
	Wife:	CATALINA ARVELA		
	Son-	FRANCISCO RODRIGUEZ	age 5 months	5
	Mother-	JOSEFA ARVELA		
	Dau-	BERNARDA RODRIGUEZ	" 20 years	
1.		GERONIMO QUINTERO de AVILA		
	Wife:	MARIA MANUELA MATOS		6
	Son-	ESTEVAN QUINTERO de AVILA	9 months	
	Dau-	MARIA QUINTERO de AVILA	7 years	
	Dau-	PETROLINA QUINTERO de AVILA	5 "	
	Dau-	JOSEFA QUINTERO de AVILA	5 "	
1.		JUAN JOSEF REVERON		
	Wife:	ANTONIA de GRACIAS DELGADO		2
1.		MANUEL FRANCISCO GARCIA		
	Wife:	MARIA de ST. PEDRO		4
	Son-	AUGUSTIN GARCIA	age 10 years	
	Son-	JOSEF GARCIA	" 5 "	
1.		JOSEF GOMEZ		
	Wife:	JUANA ESMERALDO		2
				341
1.		ANTONIO HERNANDEZ		1
1.		FRANCISCO MONTESDOCCO		1
1.		JOSEF MARIA TRUXILLO		1
1.		JUAN ANTONIO GARCIA		1
1.		FRANCISCO PENA		
	Wife:	MARIA declos SANTOS		
	Son-	JUAN PENA	age 1 year	7
	Dau-	FRANCESCA PENA	" 10 "	
	Dau-	CATALINA PENA	" 5 "	
	Son-	ANTONIO PENA	" 7 "	
	Dau-	GREGORIA PENA	" 2 "	
1.		MANUEL GONZALES		
	Wife:	JOSEFA SANCHEZ		3
		FRANCESCA CABRERA		
1.		MELCHOR GARCIA		1
1.		SALVADOR RODRIGUEZ		1
1.		BARTOLOME ROMERO		1

	Armed Personnel			Total
1.	JOSEF JUSTO DIAZ			1
1.	FELIPE FRANCISCO			9
	Wife:	BERNARDA FRANCISCO		
	Son-	DOMINGO FRANCISCO	Age 18 years	
	Son-	FELIPE FRANCISCO	" 12 "	
	Son-	JOSEF FRANCISCO	" 9 "	
	Son-	LORENZO FRANCISCO	" 4 "	
	Dau-	MARIA FRANCISCA	" 23 "	
	Dau-	ROSALIA FRANCISCO	" 14 "	
	Dau-	ANDREA FRANCISCO	" 12	
1.	FRANCISCO de ORTA		"	6
	Wife:	JOSEFA LOPEZ		
	Son-	PEDRO de ORTA	" 8 "	
	Dau-	ANTONIA de ORTA	" 20 "	
	Dau-	JOSEFA de ORTA	" 11 "	
	Dau-	ISABEL de ORTA	" 10 "	
1.	MATHIAS FRANCISCO			1
1.	JOSEF DOMINGUEZ			
	Wife:	MARIA FRANCESCA		5
	Son-	FERNANDO DOMINGUEZ	" 8 "	
	Son-	TOMOSO DOMINGUEZ	" 7	
				382
1.	JUAN FRANCISCO GUSMAN			
	Sister ANTONIA		30 "	2
1.	ANTONIO GONZALES CAMACHO			
	Wife:	RITA BLANCO		2
1.	FRANCISCO BERDE			1
1.	CHRISTOVAL QUINTERO			1
1.	FRANCISCO ANTONIO HERRERA			1
1.	JOSEF HERNANDEZ CORVO			
	Wife:	BEATRICE FRANCESCA		
	Son-	SALVADOR CORVO	Age 8 years	
	Dau-	ANTONIA CORVO	" 4 "	5
	Son-	FRANCISCO CORVO	" 14 months	
1.	FRANCISCO RAMIRES			4
	Wife:	ANA PEREZ		
	Son-	FRANCISCO RAMIRES	" 4 years	
	Dau-	ANTONIA RAMIRES	" 5 months	

Armed Personnel			Total
1. TOMAS MAYOX			
Wife:	GREGORIA SANCHEZ		8
Son-	CHRISTOVAL MAYOX	Age 18 years	
Son-	JOSEF MAYOX	" 5 "	
Son-	PEDRO MÀYOX	" 3 "	
Dau-	CATALINA MAYOX	" 20 "	
Dau-	LEONOR MAYOX	" 12 "	
Dau-	MARIA MAYOX	" 6 "	
1. BARTOLOME HERNANDEZ			
Wife:	JOSEFA ORTEGA		5
Dau-	MARIA HERNANDEZ	" 7 "	
Dau-	ANA HERNANDEZ	" 4 "	
Son-	FRANCISCO HERNANDEZ	14 months	
1. DIEGO MORALES			
Wife:	JUANA MARIA		3
Son-	NICOLAS MORALES	" 1 year	
1. FRANCISCO XAVIER XENERA			
Wife:	ISABEL de ESPINOSA		3
Sister:	FELIPA	" 19 years	
1. MANUEL DOMINGUEZ			
Wife:	JUANA FRANCESCA		6
Son-	ANTONIO DOMINGUEZ	" 19 "	
Son-	AUGUSTIN DOMINGUEZ	" 18 "	
Dau-	MARIA-LUISA DOMINGUEZ	" 12 "	
Son-	JOSEF DOMINGUEZ	" 5	
			423

"SAN IGNACIO DE LOYOLA"

ABREU, Antonio Garcia, 13
ACOSTA, Maria, 17
ALEMAN, Antonio, 14
ALEMAN, Baltasar, 14
ALEMAN, Josefa, 14
ALEMAN, Juan, 14
ALEMAN, Pedro, 14
ALEMAN, Sevestiana, 14
ALFONSO, Juan Antonio, 12
ALONSO, Antonio, 17
ALONSO, Antonia, 17
ALONSO, Augustin, 17
ALONSO, Juan Antonio, 12
ANTILES, Antonio, 13
ANTILES, Juan, 13
ANTILES, Maria, 13
ANTILES, Pedro, 13
ALVARADO, Francesca Antonia, 18
ALVARADO, Juan, 18
ALVARADO, Tomas, 18
ALVARADO, Ysabel, 18
ARVELA, Catalina, 20
ASCANO, Domingo Antonio, 18
ASCANO, Juana, 19
ASCANO, Maria, 19
ASCANO, Micaela, 19
ASCANO, Pedro, 19
AVILA, Estevan, 20
AVILA, Geronimo Quintero de, 20
AVILA, Josefa, 20
AVILA, Maria de, 20
AVILA, Petrolina de, 20

BARRERO, Antonia, 19
BARRERO, Pedro, 19
BARRIOS, Barbara de, 17
BARRIOS, Diego Rafael de, 19
BARRIOS, Francesca de, 19
BARRIOS, Josef Juan de, 17
BARRIOS, Maria de, 17
BERMUDEZ, Clemento, 16
BERMUDEZ, Diego, 16
BERMUDEZ, Gregorio, 16
BERMUDEZ, Josef, 16
BERMUDEZ, Maria, 16
BLANCO, Rita, 21
BORJE, Maria, 18

CABRERA, Domingo, 19
CAMACHO, Teresa, 19
CAMBALUZ, Nicolosa, 15
CASALTA, Josefa, 13
CASANAS, Ignaçia, 13
CASIMIRO, Simon, 15
CAVALLERO, Maria, 14
CHARNERO, Domingo, 13
CHARNERO, Josef Rodriguez, 13
CHARNERO, Pedro, 13
CHOCHO, Gullermo Gonzales, 13
CHOCHO, Sebastien Gonzales, 13
CORJOLA, Juan, 21
CORVO, Antonia, 21
CORVO, Francisco, 21
CORVO, Josef Hernandez, 21
CRUZ, Juana de la, 13

DELGADO, Antonia de Gracias, 20
DELGADO, Vicente, 15
DIAZ, Augustin, 19
DIAZ, Fernando, 19
DIAZ, Francesca, 19
DIAZ, Josef Justo, 21
DIAZ, Josefa, 19
DOMINGUEZ, Agueda, 17
DOMINGUEZ, Augustin, 22
DOMINGUEZ, Antonio, 22
DOMINGUEZ, Fernando, 21
DOMINGUEZ, Josef, 21, 22
DOMINGUEZ, Juana, 22
DOMINGUEZ, Maria-Luisa, 22
DOMINGUEZ, Tomaso, 21

ESMERALDO, Antonia, 12
ESMERALDO, Juana, 20
ESPINO, Fernando, 17
ESPINO, Josef, 17
ESPINOSA, Ysabel de, 22
ESTEVES, Pablo, 12

FALCON, Antonia, 15
FALCON, Catalina, 15
FALCON, Christoval, 15
FALCON, Gaspar, 16
FALCON, Juan, 16
FALCON, Miguel, 16

INDEX

"SAN IGNACIO DE LOYOLA"

FERNANDEZ, Bartolome, 15
FERNANDEZ, Juan, 15
FERNANDEZ, Vicente, 15
FIGUEROA, Josepha, 18
FRANCISCO, Andrea, 21
FRANCISCO, Bernarda, 21
FRANCISCO, Domingo, 21
FRANCISCO, Josef, 21
FRANCISCO, Lorenzo, 21
FRANCISCO, Maria, 21
FRANCISCO, Mathias, 21
FRANCISCO, Rosalia, 21
FUENTES, Ana de, 16
FUENTES, Antonio de, 16
FUENTES, Francisco de, 16
FUENTES, Josef de, 16
FUENTES, Juan de, 16
FUENTES, Pedro de, 16

GARCIA, Augustin, 20
GARCIA, Josef, 20
GARCIA, Juan Antonio, 20
GARCIA, Manuel Francisco, 20
GARCIA, Maria, 13
GARCIA, Melchor, 20
GIL, Maria, 13
GIMONY, Bernardino, 15
GOMEZ, Josef, 20
GOMEZ, Juan, 12
GONZALES, Catalina, 15
GONZALES, Francisco, 17
GONZALES, Manuel, 20
GORDILLO, Antonio, 17
GORDILLO, Domingo, 17
GORDILLO, Francisco, 17
GORDILLO, Gonzolo, 17
GORDILLO, Josef, 17
GORDILLO, Lucas, 17
GUERRA, Angela, 12
GUSMAN, Juan Francisco, 21

HERNANDEZ, Ana, 14, 22
HERNANDEZ, Antonio, 14, 20
HERNANDEZ, Bartolome, 22
HERNANDEZ, Felix
HERNANDEZ, Francisco, 22
HERNANDEZ, Gabriel, 19
HERNANDEZ, Juan, 14
HERNANDEZ, Lorenzo, 14
HERNANDEZ, Luis, 14
HERNANDEZ, Maria, 14, 19, 22
HIDALGO, Francesca, 13
HIDALGO, Gregoro, 13
HIDALGO, Josef, 13
HIDALGO, Juan, 13
HIEDRA, Domingo, 16

JORGE, Maria, 19

LEON, Antonio de, 18
LEON, Lorenzo Rodriguez de, 18
LEON, Luis de, 18
LEON, Sevastiana de, 18
LOPEZ, Josefa, 19
LOPEZ, Juan, 15
LOPEZ, Juana, 14
LOPEZ, Maria, 15
LOPEZ, Gaspar Ortiz, 15

MACIAS, Francisco, 16
MACIAS, Josef, 16
MACIAS, Luis, 16
MACIAS, Miguel, 16

MARRERO, Maria, 12
MARTEL, Francesca Maria, 17
MARTIN, Antonia, 15
MARTIN, Antonio, 16
MARTIN, Josefa, 15
MARTIN, Juan, 15
MARTIN, Mathias, 15
MATHEO, Francesca, 16
MATOS, Maria Manuela, 20
MAYOX, Catalina, 22
MAYOX, Christoval, 22
MAYOX, Josef, 22
MAYOX, Leonor, 22
MAYOX, Maria, 22
MAYOX, Pedro, 22
MEDINA, Francesca, 16
MENDES, Felipe Antonio de las, 1
MENDES, Maria de las, 17
MESA, Christoval de, 17

INDEX

"SAN IGNACIO DE LOYOLA"

MESA, Josef, 17
MONTESDOCA, Francisco, 20
MONTESDOCO, Sevastiana, 14
MONZON, Augustina, 18
MONZON, Rita, 19
MORALES, Catalina, 14
MORALES, Diego, 22
MORALES, Domingo Vicente, 15
MORALES, Ignacia, 14
MORALES, Maria, 12, 14
MORALES, Nicolas, 22

NAVARRO, Ana, 16
NEDA, Domingo, 13
NEDA, Josef, 13
NEDA, Josefa, 13
NEDA, Maria, 13
NEDA, Mathias Hernandez, 13
NUNEZ, Bernarda, 17

OJEDA, Antonio, 18
OJEDA, Christoval, 18
OJEDA, Christoval, Jr., 18
OJEDA, Francesca, 18
OJEDA, Gregorio, 18
OJEDA, Josefa, 18
OJEDA, Juan, 18
OJEDA, Manuel, 18
OJEDA, Maria, 18
OJEDA, Rosalia, 18
OLIVARES, Maria, 13
ORTA, Antonia, 21
ORTA, Francisco, 21
ORTA, Isabel, 21
ORTA, Josefa, 21
ORTA, Pedro de, 21

PALOA, Don Ignacio, 12
PALOA, Dona Maria, 12
PALOA, Don Martin Ferry, 12
PALOA, Dona Olaya, 12
PALOA, Don Pedro, 12
PENA, Antonio, 20
PENA, Catalina, 20
PENA, Francesca, 20
PENA, Francisco, 20
PENA, Gregorio, 20
PENA, Juan, 20
PERERA, Catalina, 14
PERERA, Francesca, 14
PERERA, Isabel, 14
PERERA, Josef, 14
PERERA, Josefa, 14
PERERA, Luisa, 14
PERERA, Maria, 14
PEREZ, Antonia, 16
PEREZ, Josef Alesandro, 15
PEREZ, Marcela, 16
PEREZ, Maria, 15
PESTANO, Juan Hernandez, 12
PIMENTEL, Antonio Suerio, 12
PIMENTEL, Francesca, 12
PIMENTEL, Isabel, 12
PIMENTEL, Martial, 12
PINO, Josef del, 19
PINO, Maria del, 19

QUINTANA, Augustina, 18
QUINTANA, Catalina, 18
QUINTANA, Diego, 18
QUINTANA, Josef Angel, 18
QUINTANA, Manuel, 18
QUINTANA, Maria, 18
QUINTERO, Beatris, 15
QUINTERO, Christoval, 15
QUINTERO, Christoval, Jr., 15
QUINTERO, Maria, 15

RAMIRES, Antonia, 21
RAMIRES, Antonio, 15
RAMIRES, Francisco, 21
RAMIRES, Francisco, Jr., 21
RAMIRES, Juana, 14
RAMIRES, Maria, 14, 15, 17
RANDO, Gregorio Judas, 16
RANDO, Josef, 16
RANDO, Maria, 16
RAVELO, Domingo, 17
RAVELO, Josef, 17
RAVELO, Josefa, 17
RAVELO, Maria, 17
RAVELO, Salvador Luis, 17
RODRIGUEZ, Antonio, 19

INDEX

"SAN IGNACIO DE LOYOLA"

RODRIGUEZ, Bernarda, 20
RODRIGUEZ, Christoval, 20
RODRIGUEZ, Francesca, 19
RODRIGUEZ, Francisco, 20
RODRIGUEZ, Francisco, Jr., 20
RODRIGUEZ, Josef, 19
RODRIGUEZ, Josef Antonio, 13
RODRIGUEZ, Juan, 19
RODRIGUEZ, Maria, 12, 13, 19
RODRIGUEZ, Polonio, 19
RODRIGUEZ, Salvador, 20
ROMERO, Augustin, 19
ROMERO, Augustin, Jr., 19
ROMERO, Domingo, 19
ROMERO, Josef, 19
ROMERO, Juan, 19
ROMERO, Bartolome, 20
RUANO, Alonso, 13
RUANO, Ignacia, 13
RUANO, Isabel, 13
RUANO, Josef, 13
RUANO, Juan, 13
RUIZ, Juan, 13

SAINT PEDRO, Maria de, 20
SAMBRANA, Isabel, 13
SANCHEZ, Andrea, 14
SANCHEZ, Augustin, 16
SANCHEZ, Augustina, 13
SANCHEZ, Bartolome, 17
SANCHEZ, Felipe, 17
SANCHEZ, Francisco, 14
SANCHEZ, Francisco, Jr., 14
SANCHEZ, Gregoria, 22
SANCHEZ, Josef Perera, 14
SANCHEZ, Josefa, 20
SANCHEZ, Juan, 14
SANCHEZ, Juana, 14
SANCHEZ, Maria, 15, 17
SANCHEZ, Rita, 19
SANCHEZ, Salvador, 17
SANTANA, Maria, 14
SANTOS, Maria de los, 20
SOLIER, Joachina, 18
SUARES, Ana Maria, 12
SUARES, Antonio, 13
SUARES, Bartolome, 22
SUARES, Francisco, 13
SUARES, Juana, 13

TORRE, Maria, 12
TRUXILLO, Josef Maria, 20

VENTURA, Josef, 16
VENTURA, Josef Antonio, 16
VENTURA, Lorenza, 18
VENTURA, Maria, 16
VIERA, Andrea, 18
VIERA, Antonia, 14, 18
VIERA, Antonio, 18
VIERA, Maria, 18
VIERA, Maria Leonor, 18
VIERA, Salvador, 18
VIERA, Sevastiana, 18

XENERA, Francisco Xavier, 22
XIMINEZ, Felipe, 15
XIMINEZ, Juana, 14
XIMINEZ, Maria, 14

Note by the Author:

In order to attain emphasis of a very special caveat, the Author has directed that this Note be printed upon a page containing only the text thereof, as the Note treats with something which is often ill-understood in our country. We make reference to the constant change which has occurred over the generations in the accepted spellings of Spanish proper and familial names. This phenomena is, of course, not confined to the Spanish language, as similar language change and development is to be observed in all of the other European tongues.

A listing of proper names of antique vintage is therefore to be approached with extreme caution. Blind reliance upon present-day spellings is not recommended, and in researching records of the antiquity of the ones which now engage our attention, the scholar should always anticipate the possibility of spellings variant to the present and well-accepted spellings. Further, spellings were often not standardized, and divergent spellings were often used contemporaneously by learned writers to indicate the same proper name. Where the record used a spelling now antique we have followed the record, as is proper. The descendents of such a person might well, however, use a form which is entirely different from that recited in the record. One of the challenges of genealogical study is the task of demonstrating the two spellings designate but one lineage.

The Author

RECRUITS AND THEIR FAMILIES

WHO EMBARKED ON

OCTOBER 15, 1778

ON BOARD THE

"LA VICTORIA"

UNDER THE COMMAND OF

CAPTAIN ANDRES ORANGE

OCTOBER 15, 1778

INFANTRY REGIMENT OF LOUISIANA

Relative to the recruits in garrison who were married or single, destined for Havana so as to embark on the Polacra Espanol, named "LA VICTORIA" Captain ANDRES ORANGE for the Port of New Orleans.

	Armed Personnel		Persons	Total
1.	DON ANTONIO FERRY PALAO			1
1.	ANDRES de VEGA			
	Wife-	COSTANZA LUSAN		7
	Dau-	ROSALIA de VEGA, 10 years		
	Dau-	JUANA de VEGA, 8 "		
	Son-	ANTONIO de VEGA, 12 "		
	Dau-	MARIA de VEGA, 6 "		
	Dau-	JOSEFA de VEGA, 16 "		
1.	JUAN SUARES			
	Wife:	ELVINA LORENZO		2
1.	JUAN HERNANDEZ			
	Wife:	PETROLINA SANCHEZ		2
1.	CHRISTOVAL RAMIREZ			
	Wife:	ANA CAVALLERO		
	Son-	JOSEF RAMIREZ, age 18 years		
	Dau-	CATALINA RAMIREZ 15 "		
	Son-	FERNANDO RAMIREZ 13 "		
	Son-	PEDRO RAMIREZ 11 "		9
	Son-	FRANCISCO RAMIREZ 9 "		
	Dau-	MARIA RAMIREZ 10		
	Dau-	ANA RAMIREZ 12		
1.	PABLO SUARES			2
	Wife:	TERESA SANTANEO		
				23
1.	SEBASTIEN de NIS			
	Wife:	DONA ANA del TORO		4
	Son-	CHRISTOVAL de NIS, age 12 years		
	Dau-	ANDREA de NIS " 7 "		
1.	CHRISTOVAL BENTURA			
	Wife:	DONA JOSEFA del TORO		4
	Son-	PEDRO BENTURA, age 4 years		
	Son-	JOACHIM BENTURA " 2 "		
	Dau-	MARIA BENTURA " 2 "		

	Armed Personnel	Total
1.	MATHIAS GONZALES Wife: ISABEL RODRIGUEZ	2
1.	MIGUEL SANCHEZ Wife: ISABEL JUANA Sister-in-law- JOSEFA LUSAN	3
1.	SALVADOR PERAZA Wife: MARGARITA GUTIERREZ Son- MANUEL PERAZA, age 11 years Son- ANTONIO PERAZA " 4 " Dau- MARIA PERAZA 2 "	5
1.	MIGUEL MARTIN Wife: JOSEFA MEDINA Son- MIGUEL MARTIN, age 5 years Son- ROQUE MARTIN, " 4 "	4
1.	MIGUEL QUEVIDO Wife: MARIA SAABEDRA Dau- TOMASA QUEVIDO, age 5 years Dau- ANA QUEVIDO, " 2 "	4
1.	JOSEF FILANO Wife: MICAELA REYES Son- JUAN FILANO, age 12 years Son- JOSEF FILANO, " 9 " Son- GASPAR FILANO " 6 " Son- AUGUSTIN FILANO 3 " Dau- MARIA FILANO 2 "	7
		57
1.	SALVADOR RAMIRES Wife: JUANA PERES Son- DIEGO RAMIRES, age 13 years	3
1.	ANTONIO GONZALES Wife: JOSEFA RIVERO	2
1.	JUAN MEDINA Wife: MANUELA GONZALES Son- FERNANDO MEDINA, age 8 years	3
1.	IGNACIO RAMIRES	1
1.	TOMAS COLLADO Wife: MARIA ALLEMAN Sister: MARIA COLLADO, age 12 years	3
1.	PEDRO SANTANA	1

	Armed Personnel		Total
1.	FRANCISCO ORTEGA RAMOS		
	Wife:	TOMASA SUARES	5
	Son-	PEDRO RAMOS, age 18 years	
	Son-	BERNARDO RAMOS, 10 "	
	Dau-	JOSEFA RAMOS 14 "	
1.	JOSEF HERRERA		
	Wife:	LUCIA GONZALES	3
	Son-	IGNACIO HERRERA, age 8 years	
1.	MANUEL ROMANO		
	Sister-	MARIA ROMANO, age 17 years	2
1.	ALONSO CERDENA		
	Wife:	FRANCESCA ORTEGA	
	Son-	JUAN CERDENA, age 8 years	7
	Son-	FRANCISCO CERDENA 2 "	
	Dau-	MARIA CERDENA 2 "	
	Son-	JOSEF CERDENA 4 "	
	Sister-in-law-	MARIA ZAVALLOS	
1.	MELCHOR XIMENEZ		
	Wife:	CATALINA PERDOMO	6
	Son-	JUAN XIMENEZ, age 8 years	
	Son-	DIEGO XIMENEZ, " 6 "	
	Dau-	JOSEFA XIMENEZ " 7 "	
	Son-	FRANCISCO XIMENEZ, 13 months	
1.	ANTONIO SANTOS		
	Wife:	MARIA del PINO	2
1.	JUAN ANTONIO SANCHEZ		
	Wife:	MARGARITA MACIAS	3
	Son-	GASPAR SANCHEZ, age 18 months	
1.	JUAN VIERA		
	Wife:	DOMINOA OJEDA	5
	Dau-	MARIA VIERA, age 17 years	
	Dau-	ROSALIA VIERA " 13 "	
	Dau-	ISABEL VIERA, " 8 "	
1.	FELIPE SANCHEZ ROMERO		
	Wife:	MARIA SANCHEZ	3
	Dau-	ANDREA ROMERO, age 5 years	
1.	LUCAS MIGUEL GONZALES		
	Wife:	ISABEL NAVARRO	4
	Dau-	MANUELA GONZALES, age 9 years	
	Son-	JOSEF GONZALES, " 4 "	

Armed Personnel	Total
1. PEDRO JORGE CALLERO	
Wife: MARIA GONZALES	7
Son- DOMINGO CALLERO, age 4 years	
Dau- ANDREA CALLERO, " 7 "	
Dau- JUANA CALLERO, " 5 "	
Son- MIGUEL CALLERO " 9 months	
Mother-in-law, JOSEFA GONZALES	
1. DOMINGO LOPEZ	
Sister- FRANCESCA LOPEZ, age 26 years	2
1. BARTOLEME LOPEZ	
Sister- CATALINA LOPEZ, age 10 years	2
1. JUAN ALONSO ROMERO	
Wife: MARIA JORGE	
Son- JUAN ROMERO age 13 years	8
Son- FRANCISCO ROMERO " 4 "	
Son- ANTONIO ROMERO " 2 "	
Dau- ROSALIA ROMERO " 7 "	
Dau- ANDREA ROMERO " 5 "	
Dau- MARIA ROMERO " 7 months	
1. SALVADOR MILAN	
Wife: ANTONIA ALLEMAN	3
Dau- MARIA MILAN, age 10 months	
	134
1. FRANCISCO RODRIGUEZ	
Wife: ANA ROMERO	5
Dau- AUGUSTINA RODRIGUEZ, age 4 years	
Dau- SEVASTIANA RODRIGUEZ " 10 months	
Sister- JUANA RODRIGUEZ, age 20 years	
1. GASPAR SANCHEZ	
Wife: BEATRIS FLORES	
Dau- ANA SANCHEZ, age 10 years	
Son- CHRISTOVAL SANCHEZ, age 6 years	6
Son- FRANCISCO SANCHEZ, " 4 "	
Sister-in-law- JOSEFA PEREZ, age 16 years	
1. VICENTE SARDINA	
Wife: RITA GABRIELA	
Dau- MARIA SARDINA, age 13 years	4
Son- JOSEF SARDINA, " 2 months	
1. MATHIAS DIAZ MARINO	
Wife: MARIA MARRERO	
Son- JOSEF MARINO, age 12 years	5
Dau- FRANCESCA MARINO 14 "	
Dau- PAULA MARINO 10 "	

	Armed Personnel			Total
1.	GREGORIO DURAN			
	Wife:	ANA HIDALGO		
	Son-	Francisco,	age 12 years	
	Son-	MIGUEL	" 7 "	7
	Son-	JOSEF	" 6 "	
	Dau-	MARIA	" 13 "	
	Dau-	ANTONIA	" 3 "	
1.	BARTOLOME PEREZ			
	Sister-	JULIANA		2
1.	ANTONIO ACOSTA			
	Wife:	MARIA PEREZ		8
	Dau-	ANDREA ACOSTA	18 years	
	Son-	LORENZO ACOSTA	14 "	
	Son-	DOMINGO ACOSTA	13 "	
	Son-	FRANCISCO ACOSTA	10 "	
	Son-	BLAS ACOSTA	8 "	
	Dau-	MARIA ACOSTA	15 months	
1.	BARTOLOME DIAZ 2º			
	Wife:	JOSEFA PEREZ		
	Son-	DIEGO DIAZ	age 10 years	
	Son-	MANUELA DIAZ	" 8 "	8
	Son-	JUAN DIAZ	" 6 "	
	Son-	FRANCISCO DIAZ	2 "	
	Dau-	FRANCESCA DIAZ	13 months	
	Son-	JOSEF DIAZ	4 years	
1.	ANDRES PERERA			
	Wife:	MARIA del ROSARIO		
	Son-	ANTONIO PERERA	4 years	
	Son-	DOMINGO PERERA	2	4
1.	JUAN de LEON RODRIGUEZ			
	Wife:	JOSEFA RODRIGUEZ		
	Son-	JOSEF RODRIGUEZ	age 12 years	
	Son-	FRANCISCO RODRIGUEZ	" 9 "	
	Son-	JUAN RODRIGUEZ	" 7 "	8
	Son-	ANTONIO RODRIGUEZ	" 5 "	
	Son-	DOMINGO RODRIGUEZ	" 4 mo.	
	Dau-	CATALINA RODRIGUEZ	" 10 years	
1.	ANTONIO GONZALES			
	Wife:	ROSALIA ORTEGA		
	Son-	JOSEF GONZALES	age 8 years	6
	Son-	FRANCISCO GONZALES	" 4 "	
	Dau-	MARIA GONZALES	" 12 mo.	
	Sister-in-law	JOSEFA ORTEGA		
1.	FRANCISCO SUARES			
	Wife:	FRANCESCA SUARES		
	Son-	PABLO SUARES	age 18 years	4
	Dau-	JUANA SUARES	" 14 "	

	Armed Personnel			Total
1.	BARTOLOME MARRERO			
	Wife:	JOSEFA SOSA		5
	Dau-	TOMASA MARRERO	age 20 years	
	Dau-	MARIA MARRERO	" 17 "	
	Dau-	CATALINA MARRERO	" 14 "	
1.	FRANCISCO MONZON			
	Wife:	JOSEFA de CASTRO		2
1.	JUAN SANCHEZ MELIAN			
	Wife:	CATALINA NAVARRO		3
	Son-	FRANCISCO MELIAN	age 5 months	
1.	ROQUE de AVILA BORDON			2
	Son:	JOSEF de AVILA BORDON	" 8 years	
1.	SEVASTIAN HERNANDEZ			
	Wife:	TERESA LOPEZ		
	Son-	SEVASTIAN HERNANDEZ	" 17 "	
	Son-	MANUEL HERNANDEZ	15 "	9
	Son-	VICENTE HERNANDEZ	" 10 "	
	Son-	LAZARO HERNANDEZ	" 7 "	
	Son-	BARTOLOME HERNANDEZ	" 5 "	
	Son-	JUAN HERNANDEZ	" 4 "	
	Dau-	ANA HERNANDEZ	" 1 "	
1.	FRANCISCO CAZORLA			1
1.	ANTONIO CAZORLA			
	Wife:	FRANCESCA RUANO		
	Son-	JOSEF CAZORLA	" 14 "	9
	Son-	DIEGO CAZORLA	" 11 "	
	Son-	DIEGO ANTONIO CAZORLA	" 9 "	
	Dau-	JOSEFA CAZORLA	" 20 "	
	Dau-	MARIA CAZORLA	" 16 "	
	Dau-	CATALINA CAZORLA	" 4 "	
	Dau-	ROSALIA CAZORLA	9 months	
1.	LORENZO HUERTA			1
1.	RAMON de CUBAS			1
1.	MANUEL MELO			1
1.	PATRICIO MELO			1
1.	PEDRO GUEDES			
	Wife:	ISABEL de SOSA		4
	Dau-	SEVASTIANA GUEDES	age 22 years	
	Son-	JOSEF GUEDES	" 7 "	
1.	DOMINGO MELO			1

	Armed Personnel		Total
1.	MELCHOR DIAZ DONOSO		1
1.	PEDRO SELOS REYES		1
1.	SEVASTIAN LOPEZ		1
1.	LUCAS AUGUSTIN SANTANA		1
1.	FRANCISCO LOPEZ MACHADO		
	Wife: MARGARITA RAMIRES		3
	Dau- MARIA MACHADO	age 3 months	
1.	FERNANDO RODRIGUEZ		
	Wife: RITA PERDOMO		4
	Sister- LUCIA RODRIGUEZ		
	Sister- MARIA RODRIGUEZ		
1.	JOACHIM del PINO		
	Wife: CATALINA ESPINOSA		4
	Son- JOSEF del PINO	age 3 years	
	Son- CHRISTOVAL del PINO	" 10 months	
1.	JOSEF SANCHEZ RAMIRES		1
1.	JOSEF AUGUSTIN HENRRIQUE		1
1.	JUAN GONZALES SUERIO		
	Wife: CATALINA ESPINOSA		
	Dau- ANA SUERIO	age 12 years	
	Son- ANTONIO SUERIO	" 4 "	
1.	BARTOLOME HERNANDEZ HIDALGO		2
	Wife: ISABEL HIDALGO		
1.	ANTONIO MARTEL		
	Wife: FRANCESCA ANTONIA		
	Son- ANTONIO MARTEL	" 6 "	
	Son- DOMINGO MARTEL	" 2 "	5
	Dau- BLAVINA MARTEL	" 11 "	
1.	SALVADOR BERMUDES		
	Wife: MARIA RAMOS		2
1.	MIGUEL ESPINO		1
1.	JOACHIM DIAZ		2
	Wife: JOSEFA ANA		
1.	JUAN DIAZ		1
1.	JOACHIM del PINO		2
	Brother- FRANCISCO del PINO		

	Armed Personnel	Total
1.	JOSEF MATHEO	1
1.	DIEGO GONZALES	1
1.	JOSEF GONZALES Sister: CATALINA GONZALES	2
1.	BLAS ALEMAN	1
1.	JUAN del PINO RODRIGUEZ	1
		283

INDEX

"LA VICTORIA"

ACOSTA, Andrea, 33
ACOSTA, Antonio, 33
ACOSTA, Blas, 33
ACOSTA, Domingo, 33
ACOSTA, Francisco, 33
ACOSTA, Lorenzo, 33
ACOSTA, Maria, 33
ALEMAN, Blas, 36
ALLEMAN, Antonia, 32

BENTURA, Christoval, 29
BENTURA, Joaquim, 29
BENTURA, Maria, 29
BENTURA, Pedro, 29
BERMUDES, Salvador, 35
BORDON, Roque de Avila, 34

CALLERO, Andrea, 32
CALLERO, Domingo, 32
CALLERO, Juana, 32
CALLERO, Maria, 32
CALLERO, Miguel, 32
CASTRO, Josefa de, 34
CAZORLA, Antonio, 34
CAZORLA, Catalina, 34
CAZORLA, Diego, 34
CAZORLA, Diego Antonio, 34
CAZORLA, Francisco, 34
CAZORLA, Josef, 34
CAZORLA, Maria, 34
CAZORLA, Rosalia, 34
CAVALLERO, Ana, 29
CERDENA, Alonso, 31
CERDENA, Francesca, 31
CERDENA, Francisco, 31
CERDENA, Losef, 31
CERDENA, Juan, 31
CERDENA, Maria, 31
COLLADO, Tomas, 30
CUBAS, Ramon de, 34

DIAZ, Bartolome, 33
DIAZ, Diego, 33
DIAZ, Francesca, 33
DIAZ, Francisco, 33
DIAZ, Josef, 33
DIAZ, Juan, 33, 35
DIAZ, Manuela, 33
DONOSO, Melchor Diaz, 35
DURAN, Gregorio, 33

ESPINO, Miguel, 35
ESPINOSO, Catalina, 35

FILANO, Augustin, 30
FILANO, Gaspar, 30
FILANO, Josef, 30
FILANO, Josef, Jr., 30
FILANO, Juan, 30
FLORES, Beatris, 32

GABRIELA, Rita, 32
GONZALES, Antonio, 30, 33
GONZALES, Catalina, 36
GONZALES, Diego, 36
GONZALES, Francisco, 33
GONZALES, Josef, 31, 33
GONZALES, Isabel, 31
GONZALES, Lucia, 31
GONZALES, Manuela, 30
GONZALES, Maria, 32, 33
GONZALES, Mathias, 30
GONZALES, Miguel, 31
GUEDES, Josef, 34
GUEDES, Pedro, 34
GUEDES, Sevastiana, 34
GUTIERREZ, Margarita, 30

HENRIQUE, Josef Augustin, 35
HERNANDEZ, Ana, 34
HERNANDEZ, Bartolome, 34
HERNANDEZ, Juan, 34
HERNANDEZ, Lazaro, 34
HERNANDEZ, Manuel, 34
HERNANDEZ, Sevastian, 34
HERNANDEZ, Sevastian, Jr., 34
HERRERA, Ignacio, 31
HERRERA, Josef, 31
HIDALGO, Ana, 33
HIDALGO, Bartolome Hernandez, 35
HIDALGO, Isabel, 35

JORGE, Maria, 32

LOPEZ, Bartolome, 32
LOPEZ, Catalina, 32
LOPEZ, Domingo, 32
LOPEZ, Francesca, 32
LOPEZ, Teresa, 34
LOPEZ, Sevastien, 35

INDEX
"LA VICTORIA"

MACHADO, Francisco Lopez, 35
MACHADO, Maria, 35
MARINO, Francesca, 32
MARINO, Josef, 32
MARINO, Mathias Diaz, 32
MARINO, Paula, 32
MARTEL, Antonio, 35
MARTEL, Blavina, 35
MARTEL, Domingo, 35
MARRERO, Bartolome, 34
MARRERO, Catalina, 34
MARRERO, Maria, 32, 34
MARRERO, Tomaso, 34
MARTIN, Miguel, 30
MARTIN, Miguel, Jr., 30
MARTIN, Rocque, 30
MATHEO, Josef, 35
MEDINA, Fernando, 30
MEDINA, Josefa, 30
MELIAN, Francisco, 34
MELIAN, Juan Sanchez, 34
MELO, Domingo, 34
MELO, Manuel, 34
MELO, Patricio, 34
MILAN, Maria, 32
MILAN, Salvador, 32
MONZON, Francisco, 34
NIS, Andrea de, 29
NIS, Christoval de, 29
NIS, Sevastien de, 29
NAVARRO, Isabel, 31
OJEDA, Dominos, 31
ORTEGA, Rosalia, 33
PALAO, Don Antonio Ferry, 29
PERDOMO, Catalina, 31
PERDOMO, Rita, 35
PERERA, Andres, 33
PERERA, Antonio, 33
PERERA, Domingo, 33
PEREZ, Bartolome, 33
PEREZ, Josefa, 33
PEREZ, Juliana, 33
PERAZA, Antonio, 30
PEREZA, Manuel, 30
PEREZA, Maria, 30
PERAZA, Salvador, 30
PINO, Christoval del, 35
PINO, Francisco, del, 35
PINO, Joaquim del, 35
PINO, Josef del, 35
QUEVIDO, Ana, 30
QUEVIDO, Miguel, 30
QUEVIDO, Tomasa, 30
RAMIREZ, Ana, 29
RAMIREZ, Catalina, 29
RAMIREZ, Christoval, 29
RAMIREZ, Diego, 30
RAMIREZ, Fernando, 29
RAMIREZ, Francisco, 29
RAMIREZ, Ignacio, 30
RAMIREZ, Josef, 29
RAMIREZ, Josef Sanchez, 35
RAMIREZ, Margarita, 35
RAMIREZ, Maria, 29
RAMIREZ, Pedro, 29
RAMIREZ, Salvador, 30
RAMOS, Bernardo, 31
RAMOS, Francisco Ortega, 31
RAMOS, Josefa, 31
RAMOS, Pedro, 31
RAMOS, Maria, 35
REYNES, Micaela, 30
REYNES, Pedro Selos, 35
RODRIGUEZ, Antonio, 33
RODRIGUEZ, Augustina, 32
RODRIGUEZ, Catalina, 33
RODRIGUEZ, Domingo, 33
RODRIGUEZ, Francisco, 32, 33
RODRIGUEZ, Isabel, 30
RODRIGUEZ, Josef, 33
RODRIGUEZ, Josefa, 33
RODRIGUEZ, Juan, 33
RODRIGUEZ, Juan de Leon, 33
RODRIGUEZ, Juan del Pino, 36
RODRIGUEZ, Juana, 32
RODRIGUEZ, Lucia, 35
RODRIGUEZ, Maria, 35
RODRIGUEZ, Sevastiana, 32
ROMANO, Manuel, 31
ROMANO, Maria, 31
ROMERO, Ana, 32
ROMERO, Andrea, 31, 32
ROMERO, Antonio, 32
ROMERO, Felipe Sanchez, 31
ROMERO, Francisco, 32
ROMERO, Juan, 32
ROMERO, Juan Alonso, 32
ROMERO, Maria, 32
ROMERO, Rosalia, 32
ROSARIO, Maria del, 33

INDEX

"LA VICTORIA"

SAABEDRA, Maria, 30
SANCHEZ, Ana, 32
SANCHEZ, Christoval, 32
SANCHEZ, Francisco, 32
SANCHEZ, Gaspar, 31, 32
SANCHEZ, Juan Antonio, 31
SANCHEZ, Maria, 31
SANCHEZ, Miguel, 30
SANTANA, Luis Augustin, 35
SANTANA, Pedro, 30
SANTOS, Antonio, 31
SARDINA, Josef, 32
SARDINA, Maria, 32
SARDINA, Vivente, 32
SOSA, Isabel de, 34
SOSA, Josefa de, 34
SUARES, Francesca, 33
SUARES, Francisco, 33
SUARES, Juan, 29
SUARES, Juana, 33
SUARES, Pablo, 29, 33
SUARES, Tomaso, 31
SUERIO, Ana, 35
SUERIO, Antonio, 35
SUERIO, Juan Gonzales, 35

TORO, Dona Ana del, 29
TORO, Dona Josefa del, 29

VEGA, Andres de, 29
VEGA, Antonio de, 29
VEGA, Josefa de, 29
VEGA, Juana de, 29
VEGA, Maria de, 29
VEGA, Rosalia de, 29
VIERA, Isabel, 31
VIERA, Juam, 31
VIERA, Maria, 31
VIERA, Rosalia, 31

XIMINEZ, Diego, 31
XIMINEZ, Francisco, 31
XIMINEZ, Josefa, 31
XIMINEZ, Juan, 31
XIMINEZ, Melchor, 31

RECRUITS AND THEIR FAMILIES

WHO EMBARKED ON

DECEMBER 9, 1778

ON BOARD THE

"SAN JUAN NEPOMUCENO"

UNDER THE COMMAND OF

CAPTAIN DON DOMINGO MORERA

DECEMBER 9, 1778

INFANTRY REGIMENT OF LOUISIANA

Relatives to the recruits in garrison who were married or single, destined for Havana so as to embark on December 9, 1778 for the Port of New Orleans on the Spanish packer, named "SAN JUAN NEPOMUCENO". CAPTAIN DON DOMINGO MORERA.

	Armed Personnel				Total
1.	DON JOSEF ANTONIO HERRERA				1
1.	JOSEF GOMEZ				
	Wife:	CATALINA PERARA			
	Dau-	ANA GOMEZ	age	4 years	5
	Son-	DOMINGO GOMEZ	"	3 "	
	Dau-	MARIA GOMEZ	"	2 "	
1.	FERNANDO MORALES				
	Wife:	BERNARDA GONZALES			4
	Son-	ISIDRO MORALES		1 month	
	Son-	FERNANDO MORALES	"	2 years	
1.	JOSEF ENRIQUE de ALMEYDA				3
	Son-	LAZARO de ALMEYDA			
	Dau-	FRANCESCA de ALMEYDA		2 years	
1.	ANTONIO JOSEF de ARMAS				
	Wife:	MARIA DELGADO			3
	Son-	DOMINGO de ARMAS	"	2 months	
1.	JOSEF SUAREZ				
	Wife:	FRANCESCA RODRIGUEZ			3
	Dau-	MARIA SUAREZ	"	3 "	
					19
1.	IGNACIO ANTONIO MATOJ				
	Wife:	JOSEFA ROMAN			2
1.	BERNARDO NIEVES				
	Wife:	MARIA RODRIGUEZ			5
	Son-	JUAN NIEVES	"	2 "	
	Sister-	ISABEL NIEVES		17 "	
		BRIGIDA			
1.	LUIS PEREZ				
	Wife:	CATALINA de SAN MATEO			2

	Armed Personnel			Total
1.	LORENZO MORALES			
	Wife:	JOSEFA RODRIGUEZ		7
	Son-	FRANCISCO MORALES	Age 15 years	
	Son-	VICENTE MORALES	" 4 "	
	Son-	MIGUEL MORALES	" 2 "	
	Dau-	AGNES MORALES	" 17 "	
	Dau-	SEVASTIANA MORALES	" 8 "	
1.	ANTONIO PEREZ			
	Wife:	CATALINA PEREZ		4
	Son-	NICOLAS PEREZ	" 8 "	
	Dau-	MARIA PEREZ	" 5 "	
1.	PEDRO SANCHEZ			
	Wife:	MARIA LOPEZ		4
	Son-	ANDRES SANCHEZ	" 2 "	
	Dau-	MARIA SANCHEZ	" 7 "	
1.	JUAN de OJEDA			
	Wife:	JOSEFA CASIMIRO		2
1.	BARTOLOME CAVALLERO			
	Wife:	MARIA ANTILES		8
	Son-	DIEGO CAVALLERO	" 17 "	
	Son-	ANTONIO CAVALLERO	" 6 "	
	Son-	BARTOLOME CAVALLERO	" 2 "	
	Dau-	MARIA CAVALLERO	" 12 "	
	Dau-	AUGUSTINA CAVALLERO	" 3 "	
	Dau-	ANDREA CAVALLERO	" 1 month	
				53
1.	MIGUEL PADILLA			
	Wife:	LUCIA ENRIQUE		3
	Mother-	MARIA PADILLA		
1.	BARTOLOME MONZON			
	Wife:	MARIA PENCIBES		7
	Son-	FRANCISCO MONZON	age 5 years	
	Dau-	YSABEL MONZON	" 4 "	
	Dau-	JUANA MONZON	" 2 "	
	Son-	JUAN MONZON	" 13 "	
	Dau-	JOSEFA MONZON	" 2 "	
1.	JUAN MORALES			
	Wife:	TERESA de JESUS		3
	Dau-	MARIA MORALES	" 2 "	
1.	DOMINGO ZAVALLOS			
	Wife:	RITA MARIA		2

Armed Personnel				Total
1.	ESTEVAN CABRERA			
	Wife:	MARIA de los NIEVES		2
1.	JOSEF ANTONIO RELEVA			
	Wife:	ANA del CARMEN		2
1.	MIGUEL SUAREZ			
	Wife:	MARIA de la CRUZ		5
	Son-	DOMINGO SUAREZ	age 11 years	
	Son-	SEVASTIAN SUAREZ	" 7 "	
	Son-	MIGUEL SUAREZ	" 1 month	
1.	ANTONIO AUGUSTIN NEZER			1
1.	MATEO RODRIGUEZ			
	Sister-	MARIA RODRIGUEZ	" 23 years	
	Sister-	BABRIELA RODRIGUEZ	" 17 "	3
				81
1.	FRANCISCO ALEMAN			
	Wife:	TOMASA BORDON		5
	Son-	SALVADOR ALEMAN	" 1 "	
	Dau-	MARIA ALEMAN	" 3 "	
	Dau-	CATALINA ALEMAN	" 12 "	
1.	SEVASTIEN PERERA			
	Wife:	MARIA MORENO		4
	Son-	PEDRO PERERA	" 2 "	
	Son-	FRANCISCO PERERA	" 1 month	
1.	ANGEL GOMEZ			
	Wife:	LAZARA MARIA		
	Son-	ANTONIO GOMEZ	" 4 years	4
	Son-	DIEGO GOMEZ	" 2 "	
1.	JUAN de PLAZENCIA			
	Wife:	JOSEFA de REYES		6
	Son-	DOMINGO PLAZENCIA	" 9 "	
	Son-	ANTONIO de PLAZENCIA	" 6 "	
	Dau-	ANDREA de PLAZENCIA	" 11 "	
	Dau-	ANTONIA de PLAZENCIA	" 2 "	
1.	GASPAR de PLAZENCIA			
	Wife:	MELCHORA BARROSO		7
	Son-	FRANCISCO de PLAZENCIA	" 13 "	
	Son-	BALTASAR de PLAZENCIA	" 2 "	
	Dau-	MARIA de PLAZENCIA	" 15 "	
	Dau-	LEONOR de PLAZENCIA	" 7 "	
	Dau-	MARIA de PLAZENCIA	" 6 "	
1.	JOSEF SUARES			1

	Armed Personnel			Total
1.	JOSEF MARIA de la PAZ			
	Wife:	MARIA BEBERA		5
	Son-	RAMON de la PAZ	Age 13 years	
	Dau-	ANTONIA de la PAZ	" 7 "	
	Dau-	EUGENIA de la PAZ	" 5 "	
				113
1.	DOMINGO TRUXILLO			
	Wife:	CATALINA MARIA		
	Son-	ANTONIO TRUXILLO	" 14 "	
	Son-	JOSEF TRUXILLO	" 6 "	6
	Son-	JUAN TRUXILLO	" 3 "	
	Dau-	MARCELINA TRUXILLO	" 7 "	
1.	JOSEF ANTONIO de la PAZ			
	Wife:	MARIA de la CONCEPCION		4
	Dau-	FRANCESCA de la PAZ	" 3 "	
	Dau-	RITA de la PAZ	" 1 "	
1.	JUAN de LUGO NAVARRE			
	Wife:	MARIA de ANSOLA		6
	Son-	ANTONIO NAVARRE	" 3 "	
	Dau-	ROSA NAVARRE	" 8 "	
	Dau-	MARIA NAVARRE	" 6 "	
	Dau-	FRANCESCA NAVARRE	" 2 months	
1.	JUAN RAFAEL TRUXILLO			
	Wife:	MARIA TERESA CABRERA		2
1.	JOSEF GARCIA AGUILAR			
	Wife:	JOSEFA MARIA GUIA		2
1.	JUAN ANTONIO de NIEBLA			
	Wife:	ROSA		
	Son-	JUAN de NIEBLA	" 15 years	7
	Son-	ANTONIO de NIEBLA	" 12 "	
	Son-	PEDRO de NIEBLA	" 16 "	
	Son-	JOSEF de NIEBLA	" 7 "	
	Son-	DOMINGO de NIEBLA		
1.	BLAS RIOS			
	Wife:	JOSEFA LEDESMA		5
	Dau-	JUANA RIOS	" 20 "	
	Dau-	NARCISA RIOS	" 8 "	
	Dau-	MARCELINA RIOS	" 12 "	
				145
1.	DOMINGO FRANCISCO ESTEVES			5
	Wife:	YSABEL GARCIA		
	Son-	FERNANDO ESTEVES	" 4 "	
	Son-	MANUEL ESTEVES	" 2 "	
	Dau-	ANTONIA ESTEVES	" 5 months	

Armed Personnel				Total
1.	ALONSO de CUBAS			
	Wife:	ANTONIA de GRACIA		3
	Son-	LORENZO de CUBAS	age 6 years	
1.	JOSEF VICENTE			
	Wife:	MARIA MERCEDES		2
1.	LORENZO de CUBAS ROMERO			
	Wife-	LUCIA SANCHEZ		
	Son-	LORENZO ROMERO	" 7 "	
	Son-	ANTONIO ROMERO	" 2 "	5
	Son-	CHRISTOVAL ROMERO	" 15 "	
1.	LEON CANSILES			
	Wife:	SEVASTIANA MORENO		
	Dau-	ANTONIA CANSILES	" 10 "	6
	Son-	JUAN CANSILES	" 7 "	
	Dau-	MARIA CANSILES	" 4 "	
	Dau-	CATALINA CANSILES	" 8 months	
1.	MANUEL RODRIGUEZ			
	Wife:	LUCIA BRITO		2
1.	CARLOS THEODORO de ACEBEDO			
	Wife:	ANA FRANCESCA FERNANDEZ		9
	Dau-	RAFAELA de ACEBEDO	" 16 years	
	Dau-	MARGARITA de ACEBEDO	" 14 "	
	Dau-	BARBARA de ACEBEDO	" 11 "	
	Son-	CARLOS de ACEBEDO	" 9 "	
	Son-	JOSEF de ACEBEDO	" 7 "	
	Dau-	MARIA de ACEBEDO	" 5 "	
	Dau-	JUANA de ACEBEDO	" 2 "	
				177
1.	SIMON VERDE			
	Wife:	ANA SANCHEZ		4
	Dau-	CATALINA VERDE	" 16 "	
	Dau-	JOSEFA VERDE	" 13 "	
1.	MATHIAS CABRERA			
	Wife:	MARIA BUTO		2
1.	RAMON LOPEZ			
	Wife:	MARIA VERDE		2
1.	ANTONIO LOPEZ			
	Wife:	CATALINA PENA		4
	Son-	JUAN LOPEZ	" 3 "	
	Son-	BERNARDO LOPEZ	" 1 "	

	Armed Personnel			Total
1.	LUCAS AGUILAR			
	Wife:	MARIA del CASTILLO		3
	Dau-	FRANCESCA del CASTILLO	age 18 years	
1.	TOMAS LORENZO			
	Wife:	MARIA del JESUS CABALLERA		
	Son-	ISIDORO LORENZO	" 6 "	
	Dau-	ESTEVANA LORENZO	" 3 "	5
	Dau-	FRANCESCA LORENZO	" 1 month	
1.	PEDRO ESPINOSA			
	Wife:	MARIA MERTEL		4
	Son-	LUIS ESPINOSA	" 8 years	
	Dau-	NARCISA ESPINOSA	" 1 month	
1.	JUAN GALAN			1
				202

INDEX

"SAN JUAN NEPOMUCENO"

ACEBEDO, Barbara de, 45
ACEBEDO, Carlos Theodoro de, 45
ACEBEDO, Carlos Theodoro de, Jr., 45
ACEBEDO, Josef de, 45
ACEBEDO, Juana, de, 45
ACEBEDO, Margarita de, 45
ACEBEDO, Rafaela de, 45
AGUILAR, Francesca de, 41
AGUILAR, Josef Garcia, 44
AGUILAR, Lucas, 46
ALEMAN, Catalina, 43
ALEMAN, Francisco, 43
ALEMAN, Maria, 43
ALEMAN, Salvador, 43
ALMEYDA, Francesca de, 41
ALMEYDA, Josef Enrique de, 41
ALMEYDA, Lazaro de, 41
ANTILES, Maria, 42
ARMAS, Antoni Josef de, 41
ARMAS, Domingo de, 41

BARROSO, Melchora, 43
BEBERA, Maria, 44
BRITO, Lucia, 45
BORDON, Tomasa, 43
BUTO, Maria, 45

CABRERA, Estevan, 43
CABRERA, Maria Teresa, 44
CANSILES, Antonio, 45
CANSILES, Catalina, 45
CANSILES, Juan, 45
CANSILES, Leon, 45
CANSILES, Maria, 45
CASTILLO, Maria del, 46
CASIMIRO, Josefa, 42
CAVALLERO, Abdrea, 42
CAVALLERO, Antonio, 42
CAVALLERO, Bartolome, 42
CAVALLERO, Diego, 42
CAVALLERO, Augustina, 42
CAVALLERO, Maria, 42
CONCEPCION, Maria de la, 44
CRUZ, Maria de la, 43

DELGADO, Maria, 41

ENRIQUE, Lucia, 42
ESPINOSA, Luis, 46
ESPINOSA, Pedro, 46
ESPINOSA, Narcisa, 46
ESTEVES, Antonia, 44
ESTEVES, Domingo, 44
ESTEVES, Fernando, 44
ESTEVES, Manuel, 44

GALAN, Juan, 46
GARCIA, Isabel, 44
GOMEZ, Angel, 43
GOMEZ, Ana, 41
GOMEZ, Diego, 43
GOMEZ, Domingo, 41
GONZALES, Bernarda, 41
GRACIA, Antonia de, 45
GUIA, Josef Maria, 44

HERRERA, Don Josef Antonio, 41

JESUS, Teresa de, 42

LODESMA, Josefa, 44
LOPEZ, Antonio, 45
LOPEZ, Bernardo, 45
LOPEZ, Juan, 45
LOPEZ, Ramon, 45
LORENZO, Estevana, 46
LORENZO, Francesca, 46
LORENZO, Isidoro, 45
LORENZO, Tomas, 46

MATOJ, Ignacio Antonio, 41
MERCEDES, Maria, 45
MERTEL, Maria, 46
MONZON, Bartolome, 42
MONZON, Francisco, 42
MONZON, Isabel, 42
MONZON, Josefa, 42
MONZON, Juan, 42
MONZON, Juana, 42
MORALES, Agnes, 42
MORALES, Fernando, 41
MORALES, Fernando, Jr., 41
MORALES, Isidro, 41
MORALES, Francisco, 42
MORALES, Juan, 42
MORALES, Lorenzo, 42
MORALES, Maria, 42
MORALES, Sevastiana, 42
MORALES, Vicente, 42

INDEX
"SAN JUAN NEPOMUCENO"

MORENO, Maria, 43
MORENO, Sevastiana, 45

NAVARRE, Antonio, 44
NAVARRE, Francesca, 44
NAVARRE, Juan de Lugo, 44
NAVARRE, Maria, 44
NAVARRE, Rosa, 44
NEZER, Antonio Augustin, 43
NIEBLA, Antonio de, 44
NIEBLA, Domingo de, 44
NIEBLA, Josef de, 44
NIEBLA, Juan de, 44
NIEBLA, Juan Antonio de, 44
NIEBLA, Pedro de, 44
NIEVES, Bernardo, 41
NIEVES, Maria de los, 43

PADILLA, Maria, 42
PADILLA, Miguel, 42
PAZ, Antonio de la, 44
PAZ, Eugenia de la, 44
PAZ, Josef Maria de la, 44
PAZ, Francesca de la, 44
PAZ, Josef Antonio de la, 44
PAZ, Ramon de la, 44
PAZ, Rita de la, 44
PENA, Catalina, 45
PENCIBES, Maria, 42
PERERA, Catalina, 41
PERERA, Francisco, 43
PERERA, Pedro, 43
PERERA, Sevastien, 43
PEREZ, Antonio, 42
PEREZ, Catalina, 42
PEREZ, Maria, 42
PEREZ, Nicolas, 42
PLAZENCIA, Andrea de, 43
PLAZENCIA, Antonia de, 43
PLAZENCIA, Antonio, de, 43
PLAZENCIA, Domingo de, 43
PLAZENCIA, Francisco, de, 43
PLAZENCIA, Gaspar de, 43
PLAZENCIA, Leonor de, 43
PLAZENCIA, Maria de, 43

RELEVA, Josef Antonio, 43
REYES, Josefa de, 43
RIOS, Blas, 44
RIOS, Juana, 44
RIOS, Marcelina, 44
RIOS, Narcisa, 44
RODRIGUEZ, Francesca, 41
RODRIGUEZ, Gabriela, 43
RODRIGUEZ, Josefa, 42
RODRIGUEZ, Manuel, 45
RODRIGUEZ, Maria, 41, 43
RODRIGUEZ, Mateo, 43
ROMAN, Josefa, 41
ROMERO, Antonio, 45
ROMERO, Christoval, 45
ROMERO, Lorenzo de Cubas, 45
ROMERO, Lorenzo de Cubas, Jr.,

SANCHEZ, Ana, 45
SANCHEZ, Andres, 42
SANCHEZ, Lucia, 45
SANCHEZ, Maria, 42
SANCHEZ, Pedro, 42
SAN MATEO, Catalina de, 41
SUARES, Domingo, 43
SUARES, Josef, 41, 43
SUARES, Maria, 41
SUARES, Miguel, 43
SUARES, Miguel, Jr., 43
SUARES, Sevastian, 43

TRUXILLO, Antonio, 44
TRUXILLO, Domingo, 44
TRUXILLO, Josef, 44
TRUXILLO, Juan, 44
TRUXILLO, Marcelina, 44
TRUXILLO, Juan Rafael, 44

VERDE, Catalina, 45
VERDE, Josefa, 45
VERDE, Simon, 45
VERDE, Simon, 45
VERDE, Maria, 45

ZAVALLOS, Domingo, 42

RECRUITS AND THEIR FAMILIES

WHO EMBARKED ON

FEBRUARY 17, 1779

ON BOARD THE

"LA SANTA FAS"

UNDER THE COMMAND OF

CAPTAIN DON JOSEF MARO

FEBRUARY 17, 1779

INFANTRY REGIMENT OF LOUISIANA

Relative to the recruits in garrison who were married or single, destined for Havana so as to embark for the Port of New Orleans in the Spanish frigate named, "LA SANTA FAS".
CAPTAIN DON JOSEF MARO

	Armed Personnel			Total
1.	ANTONIO FRANQUI			
	Wife:	MARGARITA PEZERA		7
	Dau-	FRANCESCA FRANQUI	age 20 years	
	Dau-	NICOLOSA FRANQUI	" 18 "	
	Dau-	MARIA FRANQUI	" 16 "	
	Son-	JUAN FRANQUI	" 19 "	
	Son	ANTONIO FRANQUI	" 8 "	
1.	JUAN GARCIA RAIMUNDO			
	Wife:	CATALINA RODRIGUEZ		7
	Son-	MANUEL RAIMUNDO	" 2 "	
	Dau-	ANTONIA RAIMUNDO	" 12 "	
	Dau-	MARIA RAIMUNDO	" 7 "	
	Dau-	ROSA RAIMUNDO	" 4 "	
	Dau-	MARIA RAIMUNDO	" 5 "	
1.	PEDRO JOSEF ALVERTO NEGRON			
	Wife:	FRANCESCA ANTONIA MACHADO		4
	Son-	PEDRO NEGRON	" 7 months	
	Mother-in-law-	MARIA de CAMPOS		
1.	JOSEF ALVERTO NEGRON			
	Wife:	YSABEL GOMEZ		4
	Son-	PEDRO NEGRON	" 3 months	
	Dau-	MARIA NEGRON	" 2 years	
1.	ISIDRO RODRIGUEZ			
	Wife:	MARIADEL RORS		6
	Son-	JOSEF RODRIGUEZ	" 4 years	
	Dau-	GABRIELA RODRIGUEZ	" 8 "	
	Dau-	MARIA RODRIGUEZ	" 5 "	
	Dau-	ANTONIA RODRIGUEZ	" 3 months	
				28
1.	JOSEF de NEREZ CABERA			
	Wife:	JOSEFA del CASTILLO		6
	Dau-	ROSALIA CABERA	" 12 years	
	Dau-	MARIANA CABERA	" 12 "	
	Dau-	MARIA LEONOR CABERA	" 8 "	
	Dau-	BLASENA CABERA	" 2 "	

	Armed Personnel			Total
1.	PEDRO DOMINGUEZ GILLAMA			
	Wife:	CATALINA FRANCESCA NEGRON		3
	Dau-	CATALINA GILLAMA	age 7 years	
1.	JUAN ALONSO CASANOLA			
	Wife:	JOSEFA RODRIGUEZ		2
1.	GREGORIO MORZON PENON			
	Wife:	LUISA ORTEGA		4
	Son-	JUAN PENON	" 14 "	
	Son-	FRANCISCO PENON	" 7 "	
1.	DON JUAN SEGURA			
	Wife:	DONA MARIA LEON		3
	Son-	TORAN SEGURA	" 2 "	
1.	SALVADOR GONZALES			
	Wife:	MARIA PADRONA		7
	Son-	PEDRO GONZALES	" 8 "	
	Son-	JOSEF GONZALES	" 5 "	
	Son-	SALVADOR GONZALES	" 3 "	
	Son-	FRANCISCO GONZALES	" 4 "	
	Son-	MARIA de la CONCEPCION	" 2 "	
1.	NICOLAS GONZALES			1
1.	JOSEF DAVILA			1
1.	ANGEL GARCIA			2
	Wife:	AUGUSTINA GONZALES		
1.	JOSEF VIERA			
	Son-	JUAN VIERA	" 13 "	5
	Son-	FRANCISCO VIERA	" 10 "	
	Dau-	MARIA VIERA	" 23	
	Dau-	JOSEFA VIERA	" 22	
1.	DOMINGO FRANCISCO GUTIERREZ			
	Wife:	JOSEFA HERNANDEZ		5
	Son-	JOSEF GUTIERREZ	" 3 "	
	Dau-	JOSEFA AUGUSTINA GUTIERREZ	" 6	
	Son-	JOSEF GUTIERREZ	" 13 months	
1.	JUAN DIEGO MORIAN			1
				68

	Armed Personnel			Total
1.	FRANCISCO PHELIPE			
	Wife:	MARIA HERNANDEZ		5
	Son-	JOSEF PHELIPE	age 7 years	
	Son-	JUAN PHELIPE	" 4 "	
	Son-	FRANCISCO PHELIPE	" 2 "	
1.	JOSEF HERNANDEZ			
	Sister-	FRANCESCA JOSEFA	" 30 "	3
	Sister-	JUANA MARIA	" 25 "	
1.	FRANCISCO VIERA			
	Mother-	ANA PADRON		2
1.	GABRIEL ALBERTO NEGRON			
	Wife:	BEATRIZ SAA		7
	Dau-	MARIA NEGRON	" 22 "	
	Dau-	AUGUSTINA NEGRON	" 18 "	
	Dau-	LUCIA NEGRON	" 15 "	
	Dau-	THOMASA NEGRON	" 12 "	
	Dau-	MARIA NEGRON	" 3 "	
1.	MATEO HENRRIQUEZ			
	Wife:	JOSEFA VELEZ		4
	Son-	PHELIPE HENRRIQUEZ	" 13 "	
	Dau-	MARIA HENRRIQUEZ	" 2 months	
1.	DOMINGO HERNANDEZ CLARO			
	Wife:	BARBARA FRANCESCA		
	Son-	JOSEF CLARO	" 13 years	6
	Dau-	NICOLOSA CLARO	" 22 "	
	Dau-	MARIA CLARO	" 20 "	
	Dau-	FRANCESCA CLARO	" 10 "	
1.	ANTONIO GARCIA PESTANO			
	Wife:	JOSEFA RODRIGUEZ		2
1.	JUAN JOSEF GARCIA MELCHOR			
	Wife:	JOSEFA de los SANTOS		2
1.	JUAN de MENDOZA			
	Wife:	FRANCESCA RAFAELA		4
	Dau-	ANTONIA de MENDOZA	" 10 "	
	Dau-	MARIA del CARMEN	" 2 "	
1.	FRANCISCO GARCIA MELCHOR			
	Son-	ANTONIO MELCHOR	" 15 "	3
	Dau-	MARIA MELCHOR	" 23	
				106
1.	PEDRO FRANCISCO MANUEL PLAZENCIA			
	Wife:	BEATRIZ CABREROR		3
	Dau-	MARIA ROSALIA PLAZENCIA	9 "	

	Armed Personnel			Total
1.	JUAN MANUEL PLAZENCIA			
	Wife:	MARIA MENDOZA		5
	Son-	ANTONIO PLAZENCIA	age 8 years	
	Son-	PEDRO PLAZENCIA	" 2 "	
	Dau-	MARIA PLAZENCIA	" 5 "	
1.	JUAN PERDOMO			
	Wife:	SEVASTIANA de ARMAS		3
	Dau-	THERESA PERDOMO	" 19 "	
1.	ANTONIO de la CRUZ			
	Wife:	FRANCESCA THERESA		3
	Dau-	MARIA del ROSARIO de la Cruz	4 "	
1.	BERNARDO de la PAZ			
	Wife:	MARIA de AGUILAR		3
	Dau-	JUANA de la PAZ	" 5 "	
1.	AUGUSTIN DIAZ de NEDA			
	Wife:	MARIA SERAFINA de LEON		3
	Son-	AUGUSTIN de NEDA	" 5 months	
1.	ANTONIO BAROSSA			
	Wife:	FELICIANA JOSEFA de CUBAS		6
	Son-	JUAN BAROSSO	" 8 years	
	Son-	ANTONIO BAROSSO	" 5 "	
	Son-	PEDRO BAROSSA	" 5 "	
	Dau-	JOSEFA BAROSSA	" 18 "	
1.	ANTONIO JOSEF HERNANDEZ			
	Wife:	MARIA del CARMEN		2
1.	JUAN ANTONIO REYEZ			
	Wife:	JOSEFA ANTONIA		5
	Dau-	LAURENCIA REYEZ	" 8 "	
	Dau-	FRANCESCA REYEZ	" 3 "	
	Son-	ANTONIO REYEZ	" 3 months	
1.	ANTONIO RAFAEL de la PAZ			
	Wife:	MARIA del ROSARIO		5
	Son-	ANTONIO de la PAZ	" 12 years	
	Son-	FRANCISCO de la PAZ	" 6 "	
	Son-	ANTONIA de la PAZ	" 8 months	
1.	JOSEF del ALAMO			1
1.	PEDRO MENDOZA			1
1.	ANTONIO FRANCISCO de VARGAS			
	Wife:	GRACIA FRANCESCA AZEBADO		5
	Son-	JOSEF de VARGAS	" 7 years	
	Son-	FRANCISCO de VARGAS	" 3 "	
	Dau-	MARIA de VARGAS	" 3 months	
				158

Armed Personnel				Total
1.	JOSEF ANTONIO ROJAS			
	Wife:	CATALINA MORALES		8
	Son-	CHRISTOVAL ROJAS	age 13 years	
	Son-	PEDRO ANTONIO ROJAS	" 10 "	
	Dau-	CATALINA GREGORIA ROJAS	" 6 "	
	Dau-	MARIA ROJAS	" 6 "	
	Dau-	FRANCESCA ROJAS	" 3 "	
	Dau-	ANTONIA ROJAS	" 3 months	
1.	NICOLAS de ROJAS			
	Wife:	ANTONIA de ROXAS		2
1.	DON HILARION de la PAZ BARROSO			
	Wife:	JOSEFA SALAZAR		
	Dau-	MARIA de la PAZ BARROSO	" 7 years	4
	Son-	HILARION de la PAZ BAROSSO	3 months	
1.	FRANCISCO JOSEF de ARMAS			
	Wife:	ANA FRANCESCA		2
1.	IGNACIO MARTIN MORALES			
	Wife:	RAFAELA de TORRES		5
	Son-	ANTONIO MORALES	" 8 years	
	Son-	JOSEF MORALES	" 4 "	
	Son-	MATEO MORALES	" 1 month	
1.	BENITO FRANCISCO SUAREZ			1
1.	JOSEF JOACHIM de ROJAS			1
1.	JUAN RODRIGUEZ MINA			
	Wife:	JOSEFA de ORTA		3
	Sister-in-law-	FRANCESCA de ORTA SUEGRA		
1.	PHELIPE JUAN BORJAS			
	Sister-	MARIA FRANCESCA BORJAS		2
1.	ROQUE JOSEF PERERA			
	Wife:	JOSEFA HERNANDEZ		4
	Dau-	JUANA PERERA	" 2 years	
	Dau-	ANTONIA PERERA	" 1 month	
1.	ANTONIO ROMO y AGUILAR			
	Wife:	CATALINA de JESUS		10
	Dau-	ANTONIA y AGUILAR	" 12 years	
	Son-	ANDRES y AGUILAR	" 10 "	
	Son-	BERNARDINO y AGUILAR	" 18 "	
	Dau-	JOSEFA y AGUILAR	" 17 "	
	Dau-	CATALINA ye AGUILAR	" 13 "	
	Dau-	FRANCESCA y AGUILAR	" 7 "	
	Dau-	ANTONIA y AGUILAR	" 3 "	
	Dau-	JUANA y AGUILAR	" 2 "	
				133

Armed Personnel			Total
1.	MANUEL PERON		
	Wife: ANTONIA del ROSARIO		6
	Son- SANTIAGO PERON	age 8 years	
	Son- JOSEF PERON	" 6 "	
	Dau- AUGUSTINA PERON	" 4 "	
	Dau- NICOLOSA PERON	" 2 "	
1.	ANTONIO RODRIGUEZ		
	Sister- MARIA LORENZO		2
1.	ANTONIO DIAZ		
	Mother- ANA BENITEZ		3
	Sister- ANA DIAZ	" 25 "	
1.	ANTONIO MENENDEZ		
	Wife: THERESA VICENTA		4
	Son- ANTONIO MENENDEZ	" 1 "	
	Dau- ANTONIA MENENDEZ	" 5 "	
1.	CAYETANO MENDEZ		1
1.	JOAQUIM de AGLAR		1
1.	PHELIPE GONZALEZ MANSIT		
	Wife: MARIA FRANCESCA		4
	Son- ANTONIO MANSIT	" 3	
	Son- DOMINGO MANSIT	" 13 months	
1.	TOMAS ANTONIO RODRIGUEZ		
	Wife: PETRONA PABLA de CHAVER		8
	Son- VICENTE RODRIGUEZ	" 14 years	
	Dau- GREGORIA RODRIGUEZ	" 11 "	
	Son- DOMINGO RODRIGUEZ		
	Dau- BARBARA RODRIGUEZ	" 17 "	
	Dau- ANTONIA RODRIGUEZ	" 9 "	
	Dau- GERTRUDO RODRIGUEZ	" 1 "	
1.	PHELIPE LUIS ALONSO		
	Wife: MARIA MANTA CARRERA		3
	Son- DIEGO ALONSO	" 3 "	
1.	FRANCISCO ANTONIO GONZALES		
	Wife: ANTONIA FRANCESCA ABSAR		6
	Son- FRANCISCO GONZALES	" 7 "	
	Son- LORENZO GONZALES	" 3 "	
	Dau- MARIA GONZALES	" 2 "	
	Son- PHELIPE GONZALES	" 1 month	
			234

Armed Personnel			Total
1.	CHRISTOVAL de VARGAS		
	Wife: MARIA MADELINA		3
	Son- JOSEF de VARGAS	age 3 years	
1.	ROQUE ANTONIO GONZALEZ		
	Wife: MARIA FRANCESCA		5
	Son- FRANCISCO GONZALEZ	" 9 "	
	Son- JOSEF GONZALEZ	" 4 "	
	Dau- MARIA GONZALEZ	" 1 month	
1.	FRANCISCO HERNANDEZ GUERIDO		
	Wife: BARBARA FRANCESCA		5
	Son- BERNABE GUERIDO	" 9 years	
	Son- ALESANDRO GUERIDO	" 5 "	
	Dau- JOSEFA GUERIDO	" 2 "	
1.	BERNARDO ANTONIO PISERO		
	Wife: MARIA DIAZ		3
	Dau- ROSALIA PISERO	" 6 months	
1.	DOMINGO MIGUEL RODRIGUEZ		
	Wife: MARIA de la GUERIDO		6
	Son- BERNABE RODRIGUEZ	" 2 years	
	Son- FRANCISCO RODRIGUEZ	" 3 "	
	Son- ANTONIO RODRIGUEZ	" 7 "	
	Dau- JOSEFA RODRIGUEZ	" 1 month	
1.	FRANCISCO ALVAREZ		
	Wife: JOSEFA de BORJAS		5
	Son- JOSEF ALVAREZ	" 8 years	
	Dau- ANTONIA ALVAREZ	" 5 "	
	Dau- MARIA ALVAREZ	" 1 "	
1.	NICOLAS de TORRES		
	Wife: MARIA DELGADO		5
	Son- JOSEF NICOLAS de TORRES	8 "	
	Dau- MARIA de TORRES	" 5 "	
	Dau- BEATRIS de TORRES	" 3 "	
1.	JUAN de TORRES		
	Wife: MARIA DE ABREU		5
	Son- JUAN JOSEF de TORRES	" 7 "	
	Son- BARTOLOME de TORRES	" 2 "	
	Dau- MARIA JOSEFA de TORRES	" 4 "	
1.	DOMINGO HERNANDEZ SOCAR		
	Wife: ANGELOR FRANCESCA MANCIT		5
	Son- DOMINGO SOCAR	" 12 "	
	Dau- MARIA SOCAR	" 14 "	
	Dau- JOSEFA SOCAR	" 10 "	
			276

Armed Personnel			Total
1.	BERNARDO LUIS ALONSO		
	Wife: BERNARDA FRANCESCA MANCIT		4
	Dau- MARIA ALONSO	Age 2 years	
	Dau- BARBARA ALONSO	" 1 month	
1.	JOSEF LUIS HERNANDEZ		
	Wife: CLARA MENDOZA		7
	Son- JOSEF HERNANDEZ	" 6 years	
	Son- FRANCISCO HERNANDEZ	" 4 "	
	Son- DOMINGO HERNANDEZ	" 2 "	
	Dau- MARIA HERNANDEZ	" 10 "	
	Dau- JOSEFA HERNANDEZ	" 8 "	
1.	AUGUSTIN MARTEL de VARGAS		
	Wife: MARIA de GRACIA CANN [a]		4
	Dau- MARIA de VARGAS	" 6 "	
	Dau- JOSEFA de VARGAS	" 1 month	
1.	PHELIPE GOMEZ		
	Wife: ISABEL FRANCESCA de AGUIAR		
	Dau- MARIA GOMEZ	" 2 years	5
	Dau- JOSEFA GOMEZ	" 2 "	
	Son- JOSEF GOMEZ	" 3 months	
1.	JOSEF HERNANDEZ		
	Wife: MARIA GERONIMA MANG [za]		4
	Son- BERNABE HERNANDEZ	" 4 years	
	Son- JOSEF HERNANDEZ	" 1 years	
1.	SALVADOR HERNANDEZ		
	Wife: RITA ANTONIA		6
	Son- DOMINGO HERNANDEZ	" 10 years	
	Son- PEDRO HERNANDEZ	" 5 "	
	Son- JOSEF HERNANDEZ	" 8 "	
	Dau- MARIA HERNANDEZ	" 8 months	
1.	CHRISTOVAL MENDOZA		
	Wife: FRANCESCA RODRIGUEZ de GUIA		3
	Dau- MARIA MENDOZA	" 3 years	
1.	ANTONIO BELLO		
	Wife: CLARA de VARGAS		3
	Son- ANTONIO BELLO	2 years	
1.	SALVADOR DIAZ		
	Wife: MARIA CASANA		5
	Dau- MARIA DIAZ	" 6 "	
	Son- FRANCISCO DIAZ	" 4 "	
	Dau- ANA DIAZ	" 2 "	
			357

	Armed Personnel			Total
1.	JOSEF DIAZ DOMINGUEZ			
	Sister-	MARIA THERESA	age 30 years	
	Sister-	BARBARA DOMINGUEZ	" 28 "	3
1.	GASPAR ANTONIO ALEOSIA			
	Wife:	ANA ALVAREZ		4
	Son-	DOMINGO ALEOSIA	" 4 "	
	Dau-	MARIA ALEOSIA	" 2 "	
1.	JOSEF GONZALES RUIZ			
	Wife:	JOSEFA MARIT		
	Son-	BERNARDO RUIZ	" 11 "	5
	Son-	DOMINGO RUIZ	" 4 "	
	Dau-	BARBARA RUIZ	" 2 "	
1.	JOSEF GONZALES VICENTE			
	Wife:	YSABEL MARIA de la LUZ		3
	Son:	GASPAR VICENTE	" 4 "	
1.	BARTOLOME MEDINA			
	Wife:	JOSEFA de GUIA		2
1.	JOSEF GONZALES de la CRUZ			
	Wife:	JUAN RODRIGUEZ CHAVEZ		
	Son-	ANTONIO de la CRUZ	" 10 "	6
	Son-	PEDRO de la CRUZ	" 6 "	
	Son-	JOSEF de la CRUZ	" 4 "	
	Son-	DIEGO de la CRUZ	" 2 "	
1.	PEDRO de TORRES			
	Wife:	JOSEFA MARIA DIAZ		6
	Son-	PEDRO de TORRES	" 8 "	
	Dau-	ANTONIA de la CONCEPCION	23 "	
	Son-	ANTONIO de TORRES	16 "	
	Dau-	MARIA de TORRES	12 "	
1.	CHRISTOVAL RODRIGUEZ			
	Wife:	MARIA FRANCESCA DIAZ		5
	Son-	FRANCISCO RODRIGUEZ	8 "	
	Son-	ANTONIO RODRIGUEZ	5 "	
	Son-	SALVADOR RODRIGUEZ	1 month	
1.	JUAN PEREZ			
	Wife:	CATALINA LOPEZ		8
	Son-	JUAN PEREZ	" 7 years	
	Son-	JUAN ANTONIO PEREZ	" 12 "	
	Son-	DOMINGO PEREZ	" 4 "	
	Dau-	MARIA PEREZ	" 20 "	
	Dau-	JOSEFA PEREZ	" 10 "	
	Dau-	FRANCESCA PEREZ	" 6 "	
				339

	Armed Personnel			Total
1.	DOMINGO LUIS RAVELO			
	Wife:	JOSEFA FRANCESCA CARONAS		5
	Son-	MIGUEL RAVELO	age 6 years	
	Son-	DOMINGO RAVELO	" 1 "	
	Dau-	MARIA RAVELO	" 5 "	
1.	CHRISTOVAL LORENZO CARRERO			
	Wife:	MANUELA MARGARITA		2
1.	JOSEF HERNANDEZ ROCAS			
	Wife:	FRANCESCA MARGARITA		3
		ANA FRANCESCA		
1.	JOSEF de TORRES			
	Mother:	MARIA BENITEZ		
	Sister-	BEATRIX de TORRES	" 25 "	
1.	MANUEL MELIAN			
	Wife:	MARIA CARRILLO		5
	Son-	ANTONIO MELIAN	" 8 "	
	Son-	ANTONIO JOSEF MELIAN	" 5 "	
	Dau-	PAULA MARIA MELIAN	" 7 "	
1.	LORENZO AZAPETA HERNANDEZ			3
	Wife:	BRIGIDA MARIA MONTESENOS		
	Dau-	ANTONIA HERNANDEZ	" 2 "	
1.	DOMINGO MANUEL HERNANDEZ			1
1.	JUAN JOSEF MONTESENOS			
	Wife:	MARIA PHELIPA LEON		2
1.	ANTONIO JUAN NAVARRO			
	Wife:	CATALINA del CHRISTO		5
	Son-	ANTONIO NAVARRO	" 4 "	
	Dau-	MARIA NAVARRO	" 8 "	
	Dau-	MARIA del PROSPERO	" 10 "	
1.	JUAN de ABREU			
	Wife:	LUSINDA MARIA TRUXILLO		5
	Son-	JUAN JOSEF de ABREU	" 11 "	
	Dau-	MARIA de ABREU	" 8 "	
	Dau-	AVA JOSEFA	" 3	
				393

	Armed Personnel			Total
1.	SALVADOR de TORRES			
	Wife:	FLORENCIA ROQ[sa]		5
	Dau-	MELCHORIA de TORRES	age 20 years	
	Dau-	JOSEFA de TORRES	" 15 "	
	Dau-	ANTONIA de TORRES	" 10 "	
1.	PEDRO LOPEZ			
	Wife:	BERNARDA PERERA		8
	Son-	SIMON ANTONIO PERERA	" 18 "	
	Son-	JOSEF ANTONIO PERERA	" 12 "	
	Dau-	ESTEFANA PERERA	" 10 "	
	Dau-	AUGUSTINA PERERA	" 8 "	
	Son-	DIEGO PERERA	" 3 "	
	Son-	PEDRO PERERA	" 3 months	
				406

	Armed Personnel		Total
1.	DIEGO RODRIGUEZ BELTRON		
	Wife:	MARIA del CARMEN	2
1.	ANTONIO SUAREZ VERA		
	Wife:	PAULA MARIA de la PAZ	6
	Son-	FRANCISCO VICENTE VERA	
	Son-	ANTONIO VERA	
	Dau-	ANTONIA VERA	
	Son-	VICENTE ANTONIO VERA	
1.	JOSEF PABLO MORALES		
	Son-	MONTAL MORALES	5
	Son-	FRANCISCO MORALES	
	Son-	ANTONIO MORALES	
	Son-	JOSEF MORALES	
1.	LORENZO ANTONIO MONTESINOS		
	Wife:	JACOBINA de la PAZ	3
	Dau-	MARIA de las MERCEDES MONTESINOS	
1.	JUAN ANTONIO de MORA		
	Wife:	BERNARDA HERRERA	7
	Son-	ALONSO de MORA	
	Son-	JOSEF de MORA	
	Dau-	MARIA de MORA	
	Dau-	ANTONIA de MORA	
	Dau-	BARBARA de MORA	
1.	JUAN LORENZO GONZALEZ		
	Wife:	MARIA ALEMAN	3
	Dau-	MARIA GONZALEZ	
1.	MATHIAS CABRAL		
	Wife:	SEVASRIANA ESPINO	2
1.	JUAN RAMIREZ		
	Wife:	JUANA LOPEZ	3
	Dau-	JOSEFA RAMIREZ	
1.	JULIEN MARRERO		
	Wife:	MARIA GONZALES	4
	Son-	JOSEF MARRERO	
	Dau-	MARIA MARRERO	
1.	ANTONIO MACHADO		
	Wife:	MARIA RAMIREZ	
	Son-	SEBASTIEN MACHADO	6
	Dau-	MARIA MACHADO	
	Dau-	JOSEFA MACHADA	
	Dau-	ANDREA MACHADA	

INDEX

"LA SANTA FAS"

ABREU, Juan de, 59
ABREU, Maria de, 56
ABSAR, Antonia Francesca, 58
AGLAR, Joaquim de, 58
AGUIAR, Isabel Francesca de, 57
AGUILAR, Andres y, 54
AGUILAR, Antonia y, 54
AGUILAR, Antonio Romo y, 54
AGUILAR, Bernardino y, 54
AGUILAR, Catalina y, 54
AGUILAR, Francesca y, 54
AGUILAR, Josefa y, 51
AGUILAR, Juana y, 54
ALAMO, Josef del, 53
ALCOSIA, Domingo, 58
ALCOSIA, Gaspar Antonio, 58
ALCOSIA, Maria, 58
ALONSO, Barbara, 57
ALONSO, Bernardo Luis, 57
ALONSO, Diego, 58
ALONSO, Maria, 57
ALONSO, Phelipe Luis, 58
ALVAREZ, Ana, 58
ALVAREZ, Antonio, 56
ALVAREZ, Francisco, 56
ALVAREZ, Josef, 56
ALVAREZ, Josefa, 56
ALVAREZ, Maria, 57
ARMAS, Francisco Josef de, 54
ARMAS, Sevastiana de, 53

BAROSSA, Antonio, 53
BAROSSA, Antonio, Jr., 53
BAROSSA, Hilarion de la Paz, 54
BAROSSA, Hilarion de la Paz Jr., 54
BAROSSA, Josefa, 53
BAROSSA, Juan, 53
BAROSSA, Maria de la Paz, 54
BAROSSA, Pedro, 53
BELLO, Antonio, 57
BELLO, Antonio Jr., 57
BELTRON, Dieogo Rodriguez, 61
BENITEZ, Ana, 58
BORJAS, Josefa de, 56
BORJAS, Maria Francesca, 54
BORJAS, Phelipe Juan, 54

CABERA, Blasena, 50
CABERA, Josef de Norez, 50
CABERA, Maria Leonor, 50
CABERA, Mariana, 50
CABERA, Rosalia, 50
CABRAL, Mathias, 61
CABREROR, Beatris, 52
CAMPOS, Maria de, 50
CANNOVA, Maria de Gracia, 57
CARONAS, Josefa, Francesca, 59
CARRERA, Maria Manta, 58
CARRERO, Christoval Lorenzo, 59
CARRILLO, Maria, 59
CASANA, Maria, 57
CASANOLA, Juan Alonso, 51
CASTILLO, Josefa del, 50
CHAVER, Petrona Pabla de, 58
CHRISTO, Catalina del, 59
CLARO, Domingo Hernandez, 52
CLARO, Francesca, 52
CLARO, Josef, 52
CLARO, Maria, 52
CLARO, Nicolosa, 52
CRUZ, Antonio de la, 56, 58
CRUZ, Diego de la, 56
CRUZ, Josef Gonzales de la, 58
CRUZ, Pedro de la, 58

DAVILA, Josef, 51
DIAZ, Ana, 57, 58
DIAZ, Antonio, 58
DIAZ, Francisco, 57
DIAZ, Josef Maria, 58
DIAZ, Maria Francesca, 58
DIAZ, Salvador, 57
DOMINGUEZ, Barbara, 58
DOMINGUEZ, Josef Diaz, 58

FRANQUI, Antonio, 50
FRANQUI, Antonio Jr., 50
FRANQUI, Francesca, 50
FRANQUI, Juan, 50
FRANQUI, Maria, 50
FRANQUI, Nicolosa, 50

GILLAMA, Catalina, 51
GILLAMA, Pedro Dominguez, 51

"LA SANTA FAS"

GOMEZ, Isabel, 50
GOMEZ, Josef, 57
GOMEZ, Josefa, 57
GOMEZ, Maria, 57
GOMEZ, Phelipe, 57
GONZALES, Augustina, 51
GONZALES, Francisco, 51, 56
GONZALES, Francisco Antonio, 55
GONZALES, Framcisco Antonio, Jr., 55
GONZALES, Josef, 51, 56
GONZALES, Lorenzo, 55
GONZALES, Maria, 51, 55, 56
GONZALES, Nicolas, 51
GONZALES, Pedro, 51
GONZALES, Roque Antonio, 56
GONZALES, Salvador, 51
GUERIDO, Alesandro, 56
GUERIDO, Bernabe, 56
GUERIDO, Francisco Hernandez, 56
GUERIDO, Josefa, 56
GUERIDO, Maria de la, 56
GUIA, Francesca Rodriguez de, 57
GUIA, Josefa de, 58
GUTIERREZ, Domingo Francisco, 51
GUTIERREZ, Josef, 51
GUTIERREZ, Josefa Augustina, 51

HERNANDEZ, Antonio, 59
HERNANDEZ, Antonio Josef, 53
HERNANDEZ, Bernabe, 57
HERNANDEZ, Domingo, 57
HERNANDEZ, Domingo Manuel, 59
HERNANDEZ, Francesca, Josefa, 52
HERNANDEZ, Francisco, 57
HERNANDEZ, Josef, 52, 57
HERNANDEZ, Josefa, 54, 57
HERNANDEZ, Juana Maria, 52
HERNANDEZ, Lorenzo Azapeta, 59
HERNANDEZ, Maria, 52, 57
HENRIQUEZ, Maria, 52
HENRIQUEZ, Mateo, 52
HENRIQUEZ, Phelipe, 52
HERRERA, Bernarda, 61

LEON, Dona Maria, 51
LEON, Maria Serafino de, 53
LEON, Maria Phelipe de, 59
LOPEZ, Augustine, 60
LOPEZ, Catalina, 58
LOPEZ, Diego, 60
LOPEZ, Estafana, 60
LOPEZ, Josef, 60
LOPEZ, Josef Antonio, 60
LOPEZ, Juana, 61
LOPEZ, Pedro, 60
LOPEZ, Josef Antonio, 60
LORENZO, Maria, 55
LUZ, Ysabel Maria de la, 58

MACHADA, Andrea, 61
MACHADA, Antonio, 61
MACHADO, Francesca Antonia, 50
MACHADO, Josefa, 61
MACHADA, Maria, 61
MANCIT, Angelor, Francesca, 56
MANCIT, Bernarda Francesca, 57
MANCIT, Antonio, 55
MANCIT, Domingo, 55
MANSIT, Phelipe Gonzales, 55
MARIT, Josefa, 58
MARRERO, Josef, 61
MARRERO, Julian, 61
MARRERO, Maria, 61
MELCHOR, Antonio, 52
MELCHOR, Francisco, Garcia, 52
MELCHOR, Maria, 52
MELION, Antonio, 59
MELION, Antonio, Josef, 59
MELION, Manuel, 59
MELIA, Paula Maria, 59
MENDOZA, Antonio de, 52
MENDOZA, Christoval, 57
MENDOZA, Juan de, 52
MENDOZA, Maria del Carmen, 52
MENDOZA, Maria Geronimo, 57
MENENDEZ, Antonio, 55
MENENDEZ, Antonio Jr., 55
MENENDEZ, Antonia, 55
MINA, Juan Rodriguez, 54
MONTESINOS, Brigida, Maria, 59
MONTESINOS, Juan Joseph, 59
MONTESINOS, Lorenzo, 61
MONTESINOS, Maria de las, 61

INDEX

"LA SANTA FAS"

MORA, Antonio de, 61
MORA, Alonso, de, 61
MORA, Barbara, de, 61
MORA, Josef de, 61
MORA, Juan Antonio de, 61
MORA, Maria de, 61
MORALES, Antonio, 54, 61
MORALES, Catalina, 54
MORALES, Francisco, 61, 54
MORALES, Ignacio Martin, 54
MORALES, Josef, 54
MORALES, Josef Pablo, 61
MORALES, Mateo, 54
MORALES, Natal, 61
MORIAN, Juan Diego, 51

NAVARRO, Antonio, 59
NAVARRO, Antonio Juan, 59
NAVARRO, Maria, 59
NAVARRO, Maria del Prospero, 59
NEDA, Augustin Diaz de, 53
NEDA, Augustin Diaz de Jr., 53
NEGRON, Augustin, 52
NEGRON, Gabriel Alberto, 52
NEGRON, Josef Alberto, 50
NEGRON, Lucia, 52
NEGRON, Maria, 50, 52
NEGRON, Pedro, 50
NEGRON, Pedro Josef Alberto, 50

PADRONA, Maria, 51
PAZ, Antonio de la, 53
PAZ, Antonio Rafael de la, 53
PAZ, Bernarda de la, 53
PAZ, Francisco de la, 53
PAZ, Jacobina de la, 61
PAZ, Juana de la, 54
PAZ, Paula Maria de la, 61
PERDOMO, Juan, 53
PERDOMA, Teresa, 53
PERERA, Antonia, 54
PERERA, Bernarda, 60
PERERA, Juana, 54
PERERA, Roque Josef, 54
PEREZ, Domingo, 58
PEREZ, Francesca, 58
PEREZ, Josefa, 58
PEREZ, Juan, 58
PEREZ, Juan Antonio, 58
PEREZ, Maria, 58
PERON, Augustina, 55
PERON, Francisco, 52
PERON, Josef, 55
PERON, Juan, 52, 51
PERON, Gregoria Morzon, 51
PERON, Manuel, 55
PERON, Nicolosa, 55
PERON, Santiago, 55
PEZERA, Margarita, 50
PHELIPE, Framcisco, 52
PHELIPE, Francisco Jr., 52
PHELIPE, Josef, 52
PHELIPE, Juan, 52
PISERO, Bernardo Antonio, 56
PISERO, Rosalia, 56
PLAZENCIA, Antonio, 53
PLAZENCIA, Juan Manuel, 53
PLAZENCIA, Maria, 53
PLAZENCIA, Maria Rosalia, 52
PLAZEMCIA, Pedro, 53
PLAZENCIA, Pedro, Francisco, Manuel

RAIMUNDO, Antonio, 50
RAIMUNDO, Juan Garcia, 50
RAIMUNDO, Maria, 50
RAIMUNDO, Manuel, 50
RAIMUNDO, Nicolosa, 50
RAIMUNDO, Rosa, 50
RAMIREZ, Maria, 61
RAVELO, Domingo Luis, 59
RAVELO, Domingo Luis Jr., 59
RAVELO, Maria, 59
RAVELO, Miguel, 59
REYEZ, Antonio, 53
REYEZ, Francesca, 53
REYEZ, Juan Antonio, 53
ROCAS, Josef Hernandez, 59
RODRIGUEZ, Antonio, 50, 55, 56, 58
RODRIGUEZ, Barbara, 55
RODRIGUEZ, Bernabe, 56
RODRIGUEZ, Christoval, 58
RODRIGUEZ, Domingo, 55
RODRIGUEZ, Domingo Miguel, 56

"LA SANTA FAS"

RODRIGUEZ, Framcisco, 56, 58
RODRIGUEZ, Gabriela, 50
RODRIGUEZ, Gertrudo, 55
RODRIGUEZ, Gregoria, 55
RODRIGUEZ, Isidro, 50
RODRIGUEZ, Josef, 50
RODRIGUEZ, Josefa, 51, 56
RODRIGUEZ, Maria, 50
RODRIGUEZ, Tomas Antonio, 55
RODRIGUEZ, Vicente, 55
ROJAS, Antonia, 54
ROJAS, Catalina Gregoria, 54
ROJAS, Christoval, 54
ROJAS, Francesca, 54
ROJAS, Josef Antonio, 54
ROJAS, Josef, Joachim, 54
ROJAS, Maria, 54
ROJAS, Nicolosa, 54
ROJAS, Pedro Antonio, 54
RORS, Mariadel, 50
ROSARIO, Antonio del, 55
ROXAS, Antonio de, 54
RUIZ, Barbara, 58
RUIZ, Bernardo, 58
RUIZ, Domingo, 58
RUIZ, Josef Gonzales, 58

SAA, Beatriz, 52
SALAZAR, Josefa, 54
SEGURA, Don Juan, 51
SEGURA, Toram, 51
SOCAR, Domingo Hernandez, 56
SOCAR, Domingo Hernandez, Jr., 56
SOCAR, Josefa, 56
SOCAR, Maria, 56
SUAREZ, Benito Framcisco, 54
SUEGRA, Francesca de Orta, 54

TORRES, Antonia de, 60
TORRES, Antonia de la Concepcion de, 58
TORRES, Antonio de, 58
TORRES, Bartolome de, 56
TORRES, Beatrix de, 56, 59
TORRES, Josef de, 59
TORRES, Josef Nicolosa de, 56
TORRES, Josefa de, 60
TORRES, Juan de, 56
TORRES, Juan Josef de, 56
TORRES, Maria de, 56, 58
TORRES, Maria Josefa de, 56
TORRES, Melchoria de, 60
TORRES, Nicolosa de, 56
TORRES, Pedro de, 58
TORRES, Pedro Jr., 58
TORRES, Salvador de, 60

VARGAS, Antonio Francisco de, 53
VARGAS, Augustin Martel de, 57
VARGAS, Christoval de, 56
VARGAS, Clara de, 57
VARGAS, Francisco de, 53
VARGAS, Josefa de, 57
VARGAS, Maria de, 53, 57
VERA, Antonio Suarez, 61
VERA, Antonio Suarez Jr., 61
VERA, Antonia, 61
VERA, Francisco Vicente, 61
VERA, Vicente Antonio, 61
VICENTE, Gaspar, 58
VICENTE, Josef Gonzales, 58
VICENTE, Teresa, 55
VIERA, Francisco, 51, 52
VIERA, Josef, 51
VIERA, Josefa, 51
VIERA, Juan, 51
VIERA, Maria, 51

RECRUITS AND THEIR FAMILIES

WHO EMBARKED ON

JUNE 5, 1779

ON BOARD THE

EL SAGRADO CORAZON de JESUS

UNDER THE COMMAND OF

CAPTAIN DON MANUEL MONGIOTY

JUNE 5, 1779

INFANTRY REGIMENT OF LOUISIANA

Relative to the recruits in garrison who were married or single, destined for Havana so as to embark for the Port of New Orleans on the Spanish frigate named, "EL SAGRADO CORAZON de JESUS" (alias la natural). CAPITAN DON MANUEL MONGIOTY

	Armed Personnel	Total
1.	DON JOAQUIM de VERA	1
1.	SALVADOR GUERRA Wife: JOSEFA MERA Son- SALVADOR GUERRA Son- JOSEF GUERRA Dau- CATALINA GUERRA Dau- IGNACIA GUERRA Dau- MARIA GUERRA Dau- YSABEL GUERRA Dau- MARIA JOSEFA GUERRA	9
1.	AUGUSTIN de SEJUS	1
1.	MANUEL RAMON Wife: MARIA SANTANA Dau- MARIA RAMON Son- JUAN RAMON Son- JOSEF RAMON	5
1.	DOMINGO MARTIN Wife: FRANCESCA de ACOSTA	3
1.	ANDRES de ACOSTA Wife: MARIA FRANCESCA FRALLO Sister- JOSEFA de ACOSTA	3
1.	ANTONIO FRANCISCO del CASTILLO Wife: JUANA MARIA HERNANDEZ Son- JUAN del CASTILLO Dau- YSABEL del CASTILLO Dau- MARIA del CASTILLO	5
1.	JUAN FRANCISCO del CASTILLO Wife: JOSEFA MARIA NEGRON	2
1.	MANUEL HERNANDEZ Wife: JOSEFA BENITEZ	

Armed Personnel	Total
JUAN HERNANDEZ	
DIEGO HERNANDEZ	6
Sister: CATALINA HERNANDEZ	
Sister-in-law- ANTONIA BENITEZ	
1. JUAN ANTONIO de la ROJA	
Wife: MARIA FRANCESCA DORTA	
Son- FRANCISCO de la ROJA	5
Son- ANTONIO de la ROJA	
Son- JOSEFA de la ROJA	
1. PIETRO PIO	
Wife: GERONIMA FRANCESCA	2
1. MIGUEL QUINTANA	
Son- MIGUEL QUINTANA	
Son- JUAN QUINTINA	3
1. LAZARO BOTELLO	
Wife: FRANCESCA OJEDA	3
Son- JOSEF BOTELLO	
1. TOMAS MENESES	
Wife: JOSEFA ANTONIA MORALES	6
Son- ANTONIO RAMON MENESES	
Dau- BARBARA ANTONIA MENESES	
Son- MANUAL ANTONIO MENESES	
1. ANTONIO VALENTIN RODRIG	
Wife: LARENCIA MARIA RAMOS	
MARIA JOSEFA, widow of the recruit,	
FRANCISCO VENTURA MONTESINOS	4
JUANA MONTESINOS, sister of deceased.	
1. FRANCISCO HERNANDEZ PALMAS	
Wife: MARIA de JESUS	7
Son- DIEGO PALMAS	
Dau- MARIA JOSEFA PALMAS	
Dau- JOSEFA PALMAS	
Dau- GREGORIA PALMAS	
Dau- FRANCESCA PALMAS	
1. FRANCISCO LUIS HERNANDEZ	
Wife: JOSEFA del ROSARIO	5
Son- JOSEF HERNANDEZ	
Dau- AUGUSTINA HERNANDEZ	
Son- DOMINGO HERNANDEZ	
1. JOSEF MEDINA	1

	Armed Personnel		Total
1.	JOSEF de ROJAS		
	Wife:	ANTONIA BINA	
	Dau-	JOSEFA de ROJAS	6
	Son-	MELCHOR de ROJAS	
	Son-	FRANCISCO de ROJAS	
	Son-	MANUEL ANDRES de ROJAS	
1.	MIGUEL MONTES DOCA		
	Wife:	MARIA FASENDA	3
	Dau-	BRIGIDA DOCA	
1.	JOSEF ANTONIO RUBIO		
	Wife:	PETRONILA de la CONCEPCION	6
	Dau-	MARIA RUBIO	
	Son-	MARCIAL FRANCISCO RUBIO	
	Dau-	LORENZA RUBIO	
	Mother-in-law-	MARIA de la CIUDAD	
1.	JOSEF GOMEZ		
	Wife:	JOSEFA ANTONIA	3
	Son-	ANTONIO GOMEZ	
1.	NICOLAS de ESTRADA		
	Wife:	JOSEFA ANTONIA	3
	Son-	ROCQUE ESTRADA	
1.	JOSEF MARRERO		
	Wife:	LORENZA CARRERO	4
	Son-	JUAN MARRERO	
	Dau-	FRANCESCA MARRERO	
1.	JUAN de AGUILAR		
	Wife:	MELCHORIA RAMOS	8
	Son-	ANTONIO CLEMENTE de AGUILAR	
	Son-	JUAN de DIOS de AGUILAR	
	Son-	THOMAS de AGUILAR	
	Dau-	BARBARA de AGUILAR	
	Dau-	FRANCESCA de AGUILAR	
	Dau-	CATALINA de AGUILAR	
1.	NTAL LUIS MOLERO		
	Wife:	JOSEFA NICOLOSA BERMEJA	10
	Son-	NTAL MOLERO	
	Son-	BARTHOLOME MOLERO	
	Son-	MANUEL MOLERO	
	Dau-	ANTONIA MOLERO	
	Dau-	AUGUSTINA MOLERO	
	Dau-	THERESA MOLERO	
	Dau-	MARIA de GRACIAS MOLERO	
	Dau-	CATHALINA MOLERO	

	Armed Personnel		Total
1.	NICOLAS ALONSO COLINO		
	Wife:	MARIA CARDENAS	3
	Son-	AUGUSTIN COLINO	
1.	MIGUEL VIL		
	Wife:	FRANCESCA de SOSA	3
	Dau-	RAFAELA VIL	
1.	BERNARDO GONZALES		
	Wife:	MARIA BETANCOURT	
	Son-	JUAN GONZALES	5
	Son-	JOSEF GONZALES	
	Son-	MIGUEL GONZALES	
1.	JUAN ALONZO GONZALES		
	Wife:	ANTONIA SUAREZ	2
1.	PEDRO SUAREZ		
	Wife:	ANDREA GONZALES	7
	Dau-	FRANCESCA SUAREZ	
	Son-	MIGUEL SUAREZ	
	Son-	JUAN SUAREZ	
	Dau-	MARIA SUAREZ	
	Dau-	MARIA del PINO SUAREZ	
1.	FRANCISCO VENTURA		
	Wife:	ANA RUINO	3
		MARIA SUAREZ	
1.	PEDRO SOCORRO		
	Wife:	MARIA HERRERA	3
	Son-	MANUEL SOCORRO	
1.	MANUEL SANDINO		
	Wife:	CATALINA PEREZ	6
	Son-	JOSEF SANDINO	
	Dau-	MARIA SANDINO	
	Son-	JOSEF SANDINO	
	Dau-	ANGELA SANDINO	
1.	NATAL RODRIGUEZ		
	Wife:	MARIA RODRIGUEZ	8
	Son-	JOSEF RODRIGUEZ	
	Dau-	TOMASA RODRIGUEZ	
	Son-	VICENTE RODRIGUEZ	
	Son-	PEDRO RODRIGUEZ	
	Son-	SEBASTIEN RODRIGUEZ	
	Son-	JUAN RODRIGUEZ	

Armed Personnel		Total
1.	ANTONIO SUAREZ	
	Wife: ANTONIA RODRIGUEZ	
	Son- DIEGO SUAREZ	5
	Son- JOSEF SUAREZ	
	Dau- MARIA SUAREZ	
1.	PEDRO ACOSTA	
	Wife: CECELIA SARDINA	4
	Dau- JOSEFA ACOSTA	
	Dau- MARIA ACOSTA	
1.	JOSEF ANTONIO COZUNA	
	Son- ANTONIO COZUNA	4
	Son- JUAN COZUNA	
	Dau- LUCIA COZUNA	
1.	ESTEVAN de VEGA	
	Wife: CATHALINA SUAREZ	5
	Son- JUAN de VEGA	
	Dau- FRANCESCA de VEGA	
	Dau- ANTONIA de VEGA	
1.	ANTONIO MIGUEL SUAREZ	
	Wife: MARIA ANTONIA SUAREZ	4
	Dau- JOSEFA SUAREZ	
	Dau- MARGARITA SUAREZ	
1.	JUAN RAMIREZ	
	Wife: MARIA PERERA	7
	Son- JOSEF RAMIREZ	
	Son- FRANCISCO RAMIREZ	
	Son- BERNARDO RAMIREZ	
	Dau- MARIA RAMIREZ	
	Dau- ANA RAMIREZ	
1.	JUAN SUAREZ	
	Wife: JUANA SUAREZ	
	Son- BARTHOLOME SUAREZ	5
	Dau- GREGORIA SUAREZ	
	Son- JOSEF SUAREZ	
1.	JUAN RODRIGUEZ ESPINO	
	Wife: ROSALIA ESPINO	5
	Bro- PEDRO ESPINO	
	Sister- MARIA ESPINO	
	Sister- JOSEFA ESPINO	
1.	FRANCISCO QUINTANA	
	Wife: MARGARITA RODRIGUEZ	2

	Armed Personnel		Total
1.	MANUEL GONZALES		
	Mother-	JOSEFA ORTEGA	4
	Sister-	JOSEFA GONZALES	
	Sister-	MARIA GONZALES	
1.	MANUEL de la CARIDAD		
	Wife:	MARIA ANTONIA SUAREZ	2
1.	JOSEF ANTONIO DUMPIERRER		
	Wife:	CATHALINA MEDINO	3
	Son-	JUAN DUMPIERRER	
1.	ANTONIO ROSALES		
	Wife:	MARIA YSABEL	2
1.	JOSEF ALEMAN		
	Wife:	ANTONIA ESPINO	5
	Son-	JUAN ALEMAN	
	Son-	MATHIAS ALEMAN	
	Dau-	YSABEL ALEMAN	
1.	DOMINGO GONZALES		
	Wife:	ANA QUINTERO	7
	Son-	JUAN GONZALES	
	Son-	MIGUEL GONZALES	
	Son-	BARTHOLOME GONZALES	
	Son-	JUAN ANDRE GONZALES	
	Dau-	MARIA GONZALES	
1.	MANUEL SANCHEZ		
	Wife:	ANA OJEDA	3
	Dau-	MARIA SANCHEZ	
1.	JOSEF LORENZO SUAREZ		
	Wife:	MARIA GONZALES	10
	Son-	ANTONIO SUAREZ	
	Son-	JUAN SUAREZ	
	Son-	MIGUEL SUAREZ	
	Son-	FRANCISCO SUAREZ	
	Son-	JOSEF SUAREZ	
	Dau-	FRANCESCA SUAREZ	
	Dau-	JUANA SUAREZ	
	Dau-	MARIA SUAREZ	
1.	JUAN ALONSO de la FUENTE		
	Wife:	BEATRIZ SOSA	
	Son-	FRANCISCO de la FUENTE	6
	Dau-	MARIA LORENZA de la FUENTE	
	Dau-	FRANCESCA de la FUENTE	
	Dau-	ANTONIA de la FUENTE	

	Armed Personnel	Total
1.	MANUEL de la NUEZ	
	Wife: FRANCESCA XAVIER	2
1.	MANUEL del PINO QUINTANA	
	Wife: JOSEFA SUAREZ	5
	Son- JUAN QUINTANA	
	Dau- ROSALIA QUINTANA	
	Son- FRANCISCO QUINTANO	
1.	JOSEF MONZON	
	Wife: YSABEL MARTIN	3
	Son- JUAN MONZON	
1.	JOSEF PEREZ LOPEZ	
	Mother- THOMASA LOPEZ	3
	Sister- JUANA LOPEZ	
1.	LUIS QUINTANA	
	YSABEL LORENZA	3
	AGNES MARIA del PINO	
1.	FRANCISCO DOMINGO ZUPA	
	Wife: ANA SUAREZ	2
1.	GASPAR LOPEZ	1
1.	FRANCISCO GARCIA	
	Wife: MARIA MAZIAS	1
	Dau- MARIA de los DOLORES GARCIA	
1.	JUAN QUINTANA	
	Wife: YSABEL MONZON	3
	Dau- MARIA QUINTANA	
1.	BARTHOLOME PEREZ	
	Wife: ANA SUAREZ	7
	Son- JOSEF PEREZ	
	Son- NATAL PEREZ	
	Son- FRANCISCO PEREZ	
	Son- BARTHOLOME PEREZ	
	Dau- MARIA PEREZ	
1.	FRANCISCO GUTTIERREZ BETANCOURT	
	Wife: MARIA RODROGUEZ	2
1.	SEBASTIEN RIVERA	1
1.	SEBASTIEN GONZALA de VEGA	
	Wife: YSABEL SUAREZ	4
	Son- BARTHOLOMEW de VEGA	
	Dau- ANGELA de VEGA	

	Armed Personnel		Total
1.	LORENZO de ARMAS		
	Sister-	SEBASTIANA MARIA de ARMAS	4
	Sister-	ROSA FRANCESCA de la PENA	
		Widow of the recruit PEDRO LORENZO	
	Son-	ANTONIO de ARMAS	
1.	JOSEF RUIZ de ARMAS		
	Wife:	FRANCESCA de VERA	7
	Son-	DOMINGO de ARMAS	
	Son-	FRANCISCO de ARMAS	
	Dau-	JOSEPHE de ARMAS	
	Dau-	ROSA de ARMAS	
	Dau-	MARIA de ARMAS	
1.	GERONIMO CUEBELO		
	Wife:	EUGENIA MARIA	3
	Sister-in-law-	MARIA ANTONIA	
1.	SALVADOR de la CRUZ CABRERA		1
1.	SANTIAGO HERNANDEZ MOLINA		
	Wife:	MARGARITA BETANCOURT	4
	Dau-	MARIA MOLINA	
	Dau-	JOSEFA MARIA MOLINA	
1.	AUGUSTIN GARCIA		1
1.	NATAL del ROSARIO		
	Wife:	ANTONIA MARIA de la CONCEPCION	4
	Son-	NATAL del ROSARIO	
	Son-	JOACHIM del ROSARIO	
1.	ANTONIO JOSEF ESTEVES		
	Wife:	ELENA MARIA de JESUS	2
1.	AUGUSTIN GIL		1
1.	JUAN ALONSO MATHIAS		1
1.	ANTONIO JOSEF SUAREZ		
	Wife:	DOROTEA RODRIGUEZ	8
	Son-	JOSEF SUAREZ	
	Son-	JUAN SUAREZ	
	Dau-	ANTONIA SUAREZ	
	Son-	LUCAS SUAREZ	
	Son-	AUGUSTIN SUAREZ	
	Dau-	MARIA VENTURA SUAREZ	
1.	JOSEF MESA		
	Wife:	JOSEFA FRANCISCO PEREZ	4
	Dau-	MARIA MESA	
	Dau-	THERESA MESA	

	Armed Personnel	Total
1.	JUAN ANTONIO MARTIN	1
1.	DOMINGO QUINTANA	1
1.	JOSEF ANTONIO de la PENA	1
1.	MATHEO CABRERA	1
1.	ANTONIO FLORES Wife: CATHALINA de ZIEPA Mother-in-law- MARGARITA de MESA	3
1.	PATRICIO GONZALES Wife: THOMASA BORJAS Son- LUIS CIRIACO GONZALES	3
1.	JOSEF LORENZO PEREZ	1
1.	JUAN SUAREZ FALCON Wife: YSABEL NAVARRO Son- CHRISTOVAL FALCON Dau- JOSEFA FALCON Dau- CATHALINA FALCON Dau- MARIA FALCON	6
1.	FRANCISCO HERNANDEZ TRUXILLO Wife: BEATRIZ HERNANDEZ Dau- JOSEFA TRUXILLO Dau- FRANCESCA TRUXILLO	4
1.	JOSEF AUGUSTIN MARTIN Wife: MARIA de REGLA Son- SEBASTIAN MARTIN Dau- ANA MARTIN	4
1.	FRANCISCO GARCIA ORAMAS Wife: FRANCESCA ACEBEDA Dau- NICOLOSA ORAMAS Son- JOSEF ORAMAS Dau- MARIA ORAMAS Son- AUGUSTIN ORAMAS	6
1.	DOMINGO MACHADO Wife: ANTONIA de LEON Dau- ANTONIA MACHADO Son- ANTONIO MACHADO Son- JOSEF MACHADO Son- FRANCISCO MACHADO	6
1.	BARTHOLOME CARABALLO	1

	Armed Personnel		Total
1.	MARCOS de ROJAS		
	Wife:	LUCIA RAMOS	
	Son-	MARCOS de ROJAS	4
	Dau-	MARIA de ROJAS	
1.	ALEXANDRO de ROJAS		
	Wife:	MARIA de la ENCARNACION	5
	Son-	JUAN de ROJAS	
	Son-	ANTONIO de ROJAS	
	Dau-	MARIA de ROJAS	
1.	SALVADOR JOSEF PINEDA		1
1.	JOSEF GONZALES LLANOS		1

Note: DONA FRANCESCA OLIVES y ESPINOSA, wife of the distinguished soldier, DON JOSEF HERRERA, who embarked on December 9, 1778.

DONA THERESA del JESUS ESPINOSA, aunt of DONA FRANCESCA, whose passage will be paid by the said niece, and the same for her sister-in-law, ELENA WOOD.

JUANA PEREZ, wife of the recruit, SALVADOR RAMIREZ who embarked on October 22, 1778, who ran away from the scene of the embarkation.

SANTA CRUZ de TENERIFE--- JUNE 5, 1779

DON ANDRES AMAT de TOROSA

INDEX

"EL SAGRADO CORAZAN de JESUS"

ACOSTA, Andres de, 67
ACOSTA, Francesca de, 67
ACOSTA, Josefa de, 67, 71
ACOSTA, Maria, 71
AGUILAR, Antonio Clemente de, 69
AGUILAR, Barbara de, 69
AGUILAR, Catalina de, 60
AGUILAR, Francesca de, 69
AGUILAR, Juan de, 69
AGUILAR, Juan de Dios de, 69
AGUILAR, Tomas de, 69
ALEMAN, Isabel, 72
ALEMAN, Josef, 72
ALEMAN, Juan, 72
ALEMAN, Mathias, 72
ARMAS, Antonio de, 74
ARMAS, Domingo de, 74
ARMAS, Francisco de, 74
ARMAS, Josef Ruiz de, 74
ARMAS, Josefa de, 74
ARMAS, Lorenzo de, 74
ARMAS, Rosa de, 74
ARMAS, Sebastiana Maria de, 74
BENITEZ, Antonio, 68
BENITEZ, Josefa, 67
BERNEJA, Josefa Nicolosa, 69
BETANCOURT, Francisco Guttierez, 73
BETANCOURT, Maria, 70
BETANCOURT, Margarita, 74
BINA, Antonio, 69
BORJAS, Tomasa, 75
BOTELLO, Josef, 68
BOTELLO, Lazaro, 68
CABRERA, Matheo, 75
CABRERA, Salvador de la Cruz, 74
CARABELLO, Bartholome, 75
CARIDAD, Manuel de la, 72
CARRERO, Lorenzo, 69
CASTILLO, Antonio Francisco del, 67
CASTILLO, Isabel del, 67
CASTILLO, Juan del, 67
CASTILLO, Juan Francisco del, 67
CASTILLO, Maria del, 67
CIUDAD, Maria de la, 69
COLINO, Augustin, 70
COLINO, Nicolosa Alonso, 70
COZUNO, Antonio, 71
COZUNA, Juan, 71
COZUNA, Josef Antoni, 71
COZUNA, Lucia, 71
CUEBELO, Geronimo, 71
DOCA, Brigida, 69
DOCA, Miguel Montes, 69
DORTA, Maria Francesca, 68
DUMPIERRER, Josef Antonio, 72
DUMPIERRER, Juan, 72
ESPINO, Antonio, 72
ESPINO, Josefa, 71
ESPINO, Huan Rodriguez, 71
ESPINO, Maria, 71
ESPINO, Pedro, 71
ESPINO, Rosalia, 71
ESPINOSA, Dona Teresa del Jesus
ESTEVES, Antonio Josef, 74
ESTRADA, Nicolosa de, 69
FALCON, Catalina, 75
FALCON, Christoval, 75
FALCON, Josefa, 75
FALCON, Juan Suarez, 75
FALCON, Maria, 75
FASENDA, Maria, 69
FRALLO, Maria Francesca, 67
FUENTE, Antonio de la, 72
FUENTE, Francesca de la, 72
FUENTE, Francisco de la, 72
FUENTE, Juan Alonso de la, 72
FUENTE, Maria Lorenza de la, 72
GARCIA, Augustin, 74
GARCIA, Francisco, 72
GARCIA, Maria de los Dolores, 73
GIL, Augustin, 74
GOMEZ, Antonio, 69
GOMEZ, Josef, 69
GONZALES, Andrea, 70
GONZALES, Bartolome, 72
GONZALES, Bernardo, 70
GONZALES, Domingo, 72
GONZALES, Josef, 70
GONZALES, Josefa, 72
GONZALES, Juan, 70, 72
GONZALES, Juan Andres, 72
GONZALES, Juan Alonso, 70
GONZALES, Luis Ciriaco, 75
GONZALES, Maria, 72

"EL SAGRADO CORAZAN de JESUS"

GONZALES, Manuel, 72
GONZALES, Miguel, 70, 72
GUERRA, Calalina, 67
GUERRA, Ignacia, 67
GUERRA, Isabel, 67
GUERRA, Josef, 67
GUERRA, Maria, 67
GUERRA, Maria Josefa, 67
GUERRA, Salvador, 67
GUERRA, Salvador Jr., 67
HERNANDEZ, Augustina, 68
HERNANDEZ, Catalina, 68
HERNANDEZ, Diego, 68
HERNANDEZ, Domingo, 68
HERNANDEZ, Francisco Luis, 68
HERNANDEZ, Josef, 68
HERNANDEZ, Juan, 68
HERNANDEZ, Juana Maria, 67
HERRERA, Don Josef, 76
HERRERA, Maria, 70
JESUS, Augustin de, 67
JESUS, Elena Maria de, 74
JESUS, Maria de, 68
LEON, Antonia de, 75
LLAMOS, Josef Gonzales, 76
LOPEZ, Gaspar, 73
LOPEZ, Josef Perez, 73
LOPEZ, Juana, 73
LOPEZ, Tomasa, 73
LORENZA, Isabel, 73
MACHADO, Antonio, 75
MACHADO, Domingo, 75
MACHADO, Francisco, 75
MACHADO, Josef, 75
MARTIN, Ana, 75
MARTIN, Isabel, 73
MARTIN, Josef Augustin, 75
MARTIN, Juan Antonio, 75
MARTIN, Sebastian, 75
MATHAIS, Juan Alonso, 74
MAZIAS, Maria, 73
MEDINO, Catalina, 72
MEDINO, Josef, 68
MENESES, Antonio Ramon, 68
MENESES, Barbara Antonia, 68
MENESES, Manuel Antonio, 68
MENESES, Tomas, 68
MERA, Josefa, 67
MESA, Margarita de, 75
MESA, Maria, 74
MOLERO, Antonio, 69
MOLERO, Augustina, 69
MOLERO, Bartolome, 69
MOLERO, Catalina, 69
MOLERO, Manuel, 60
MOLERO, Maria Gracias, 69
MOLERO, Natal Luis, 69
MOLERO, Natal Luis Jr., 69
MOLERO, Teresa, 69
MOLINA, Josefa Maria, 74
MOLINA, Maria, 74
MOLINA, Santiago Hernandez, 74
MONTESINOS, Francisco V, 68
MONTESINOS, Juana, 68
MORALES, Josefa Antonia, 68
NUEZ, Manuel de la, 73
OJEDA, Ana, 72
OJEDA, Francisco, 68
ORAMUS, Augustin, 75
ORAMUS, Francesca, 75
ORAMUS, Francisco Garcia, 75
ORAMUS, Maria, 75
ORAMUS, Nicolosa, 75
PALMAS, Diego, 68
PALMAS, Francesca, 68
PALMAS, Francisco Hernandez, 68
PALMAS, Gregoria, 68
PALMAS, Josefa, 68
PALMAS, Maria, 68
PENA, Josef Antonio de la, 75
PERRERA, Maria, 73
PEREZ, Bartolome, 73
PEREZ, Catalina, 70
PEREZ, Francisco, 73
PEREZ, Josef, 73
PEREZ, Josef Lorenzo, 75
PEREZ, Juana, 76
PEREZ, Maria, 73
PEREZ, Natal, 73
PINEDA, Salvador Josef, 76
QUINTANA, Francisco, 71, 73
QUINTANA, Juan, 68, 73

"EL SAGRADO CORAZAN de JESUS"

QUINTANA, Manuel del Pino, 73
QUINTANA, Maria, 73
QUINTANA, Miguel, 68
QUINTANA, Miguel Jr., 78
QUINTANA, Rosalia, 73
QUINTERO, Ana, 72
RAMIREZ, Ana, 71
RAMIREZ, Barbara, 71
RAMIREZ, Francisco, 71
RAMIREZ, Josef, 71
RAMIREZ, Juan, 71
RAMIREZ, Maria, 71
RAMIREZ, Salvador, 76
RAMON, Josef, 67
RAMON, Juan, 67
RAMON, Manuel, 67
RAMON, Maria, 67
RAMOS, Melchoria, 69
RIVERA, Sebastian, 73
RODRIG, Antonio Valentin, 68
RODRIGUEZ, Antonio, 71
RODRIGUEZ, Dorotea, 74
RODRIGUEZ, Josef, 70
RODRIGUEZ, Margarita, 71
RODRIGUEZ, Maria, 70, 73
RODRIGUEZ, Natal, 70
RODRIGUEZ, Pedro, 70
RODRIGUEZ, Sebastian, 70
RODRIGUEZ, Tomasa, 70
ROJA, Antonio de la, 68
ROJA, Francisco de la, 68
ROJA, Josefa de la, 69
ROJA, Juan Antonio de la, 68
ROJAS, Alexandro, de, 76
ROJAS, Antonio de, 76
ROJAS, Francisco de, 69
ROJAS, Josef de, 69
ROJAS, Josefa de, 69
ROJAS, Juan de, 76
ROJAS, Marcos de, 76
ROJAS, Marcos Jr., 76
ROJAS, Maria de, 76
ROJAS, Melchor de, 69
ROSALES, Antonio, 72
ROSARIO, Joachim del, 74
ROSARIO, Josefa del, 68
ROSARIO, Natal del, 74
ROSARIO, Natal del Jr., 74
RUBIO, Josef Antonio, 69
RUBIO, Lorenzo, 69
RUBIO, Marcial Francisco, 69
RUBIO, Maria, 69
RUINO, Ana, 70
SANCHEZ, Manuel, 72
SANCHEZ, Maria, 72
SANDINO, Angela, 70
SANDINO, Josef, 70
SANDINO, Manuel, 70
SANTANA, Maria, 67
SARDINA, Cecelia, 71
SOSA, Francesca de, 70
SUAREZ, Ana, 73
SUAREZ, Antonio, 70, 71, 72, 74
SUAREZ, Augustin, 74
SUAREZ, Bartolome, 71
SUAREZ, Catalina, 71
SUAREZ, Diego, 71
SUAREZ, Francesca, 70
SUAREZ, Gregoria, 71
SUAREZ, Isabel, 73
SUAREZ, Josef, 71, 72, 74
SUAREZ, Josef Antonio, 74
SUAREZ, Josef Lorenzo, 72
SUAREZ, Josefa, 71, 73
SUAREZ, Juan, 70, 71, 74
SUAREZ, Juana, 71
SUAREZ, Lucas, 74
SUAREZ, Margarita, 71
SUAREZ, Maria, 70, 71, 72
SUAREZ, Maria Antonia, 71, 72
SUAREZ, Maria del Pino, 70
SUAREZ, Maria Ventura, 74
SUAREZ, Manuel, 72
SUAREZ, Miguel, 72
TOROSO, Don Andres Amat de, 76
TRUXILLO, Francesca, 75
TRUXILLO, Francisco Hernandez, 75
TRUXILLO, Josefa, 75
VEGA, Angela de, 73
VEGA, Antonia de, 71
VEGA, Bartolome de, 73
VEGA, Estevan de, 71
VEGA, Francesca de, 71
VEGA, Juan de, 71
VEGA, Sevastian Gonzala de, 73
VERA, Joachim de, 27
VENTURA, Francisco, 70
VIL, Miguel, 70
VIL, Rafaela, 70
ZIEPA, Catalina de, 75
WOOD, Elena, 76

CANARY ISLAND FAMILIES WHO SETTLED
AT THE "TERRA DE BUYES" (TERRE-AUX-BOEUF)
AT A SETTLEMENT CALLED
"GALVEZTOWN y SENORA DE GALVEZ"

1779
1783

CANARY ISLAND FAMILIES WHO SETTLED AT THE TERRE-AUX-BOEUF, SAINT BERNARD PARISH, LA. 1779

JUAN de TORRES
JUAN de SEGURA
PHELIPE LUIS ALFONSO
DOMINGO MIGUEL RAMOS
AUGUSTIN MANUEL BARGAS
JOSEF ENRIQUEZ SAEA
FELIPE BARGAS
JUAN ANTONIO ALFONSO
FRANCISCO de ARMAS
ROQUE JOSEF PERRERA
JUAN ANTONIO GONZALES
FRANCISCO ALVAREZ
JOSEF GONZALEZ RUIZ
JOSEF GUERIAO
DOMINGO FRANCISCO GUERRIA
FELIPE GONZALEZ MANNITO
ROQUE ANTONIO GONZALEZ
FRANCISCO GUERIDO
DOMINGO FRANCISCO GUERRIA
SALVADOR ERMON REMEJO
FRANCISCO VIERA
CHRISTOVAL OJEDA
ANTONIO GARCIA PESTANO
IGNACIO de la PAZ
ANTONIO RAMON AGUILAR
CHRISTOVAL LORENZO CARRERO
ISIDRO RODRIGUEZ
NICOLAS de ROJAS
JOSEF ANTONIO de ROJAS
JOSEF VIERA
IGNACIO MORALES
BLAS de RIOS
JOSEF ERMANO
JUAN GARCIA
JOSEF QUINTERO
JOSEF MORALES
JUAN ANTONIO MARTIN
DOMINGO de ACOSTA
BALTASAR MARTIN
DOMINGO HERNANDEZ
MARIA ANTONIO PEREZ
JOSEF RIVERO
JUAN MEDERO
MARIA MORALES (WIDOW)
PEDRO MARTIN
DOMINGO GARCIA
NICOLAS HERNANDEZ
SEBASTIANA de NINA
ANDREA ABREU (WIDOW)
BARTOLOME HERNANDEZ

JUAN MORALES
FRANCISCO PHELIPE
DOMINGO ENRIQUEZ
MANUEL PEREZ
ALONSO de CUBAS
MATIAS CABRERA
DOMINGO de ACOSTA
PEDRO MORALES
JUAN ORTIZ ROMERO
ANTONIO de ARMAS
GASPAR SANCHEZ
MATIAS ENRIQUEZ
MANUEL OJEDA
JOSEF SUAREZ
VICENTE MORALES
DIEGO RAMIREZ
MANUEL GONZALEZ
DIEGO DUENAS
ANTONIO GONZALEZ
JUAN PEREZ
GREGORIA ERNAZ
FELIX MORERO
JOSEF AUGUSTINO
GREGORIA RAMOS
ANTONIO RAMIREZ
PEDRO GUILLES
JUAN CABRERA
VICENTE DELGADO
GREGORIA OJEDA
MELCHOR XIMINEZ
JOSEF HERRERA
GASPAR ORTIZ
PEDRO CALSINI
MARIANO GRAN
ANTONIO MONTESINO
JOSEF RODRIGUEZ
AUGUSTIN CAPITAN
JOSEF ANTONIO GONZALES
JUAN JOSEF HERRERA
AUGUSTIN PINTO
MANUEL NUNEZ
ANGEL HERNANDEZ
FRANCISCO TOLEDO
ANDRES DOMINGUEZ
JOSEF MARTIN
DOMINGO DIAZ
CHRISTOVAL RAMIREZ
ANTONIO DIAZ
JUAN SANCHEZ MELEAN
JUAN SUAREZ

CHRISTOVAL VENTURA
JOSEF FILANO
JUAN MEDINA
JUAN ANTONIO SANCHEZ
SALVADOR MILAN
JOSEF ESPINO
ANTONIO HERNANDEZ
LORENZO LOPEZ
PEDRO BARRERO
FRANCISCO PENA
FRANCISCO SUAREZ
ANTONIO (torn out)
JUAN LEON RODRIGUEZ
JOSEF ALESANDRO PEREZ
GUILLERMO GONZALEZ CHOCHO
ALONSO CARDENA
LUCAS GONZALEZ
ANTONIO PIMENTEL
ANTONIO RODRIGUEZ
BARTOLOME DIAZ
TOMAS COLLADO
MATIAS MARTIN
JOSEF PERRERA SANCHEZ
JOSEF PEREIRA
JUAN de BARRIOS
MATEO RODRIGUEZ
SEBASTIAN PERERA
JUAN JOSEF MELCHOR
ANTONIO HERNANDEZ
LORENZA AZAPITO HERRERA
JUAN ANTONIO REYES
JUAN MANUEL PLASCENCIA
ANTONIO de la PAZ
MARTIN HERNANDEZ
MANUEL GARCIA
FRANCISCO HERRERA
FRANCISCO BARCELONA
MARIA SUAREZ
DOMINGO RAMIREZ
JUAN ANTONIO MORALES
ANTONIO RODRIGUEZ
GERONIMO CASTILLO
JUAN RAMIREZ
JUAN de ACOSTA
AUGUSTIN de la ROSA
NICOLAS ESTREDA
ANTONIO MANISCO
FRANCISCO ORAMUS
DOMINGO MANSITO
MIGUEL SANABRIA
DOMINGO GONZALEZ
ANTONIO de LEON
FRANCISCO de la MAR
ANTONIO CYPRIAN
ANTONIO MEDINA
JUAN ALEMAN
ANTONIO RUBIO

MIGUEL MARTIN
SALVADOR RAMIREZ
ANTONIO SANTOS
JUAN VIERA
FRANCISCO RODRIGUEZ
JUAN GONZALEZ SUERIO
DIEGO MORALES
FELIPE MERCEDES
CHRISTOVAL MESA
TOMAS (torn out)
JOSEF (torn out)
FRANCISCO MARZON
JUAN HERNANDEZ
LUIS MACIAS
FRANCISCO SANCHEZ MILEAN
JOSEF ROMERO
GREGORIO DURAN
MANUEL FRANCISCO GARCIA
VICENTE SANDINO
JOSEF de la SANTA
JOSEF del PINO
JOSEF MORALES
JOSEF BERMUDEZ
SALVADOR VIERA
JUAN SANCHEZ
RAMON LOPEZ
LORENZA ROMERO
MAURECIO GARCIA MELCHOR
ANTONIO MANUEL NAVARRO
PABLO ESTEVES
ANTONIO BARROSO
AUGUSTIN DIAZ de NOYA
CHRISTOVAL MENDOZA
GREGORIA GONZALEZ
JULIAN BUNO
JOSEF ROBERA
JUAN ANGEL
FRANCISCO de la MAR
DOMINGO ANTONIO CABRERA
JOSEF ANTONIO MARTINEZ
MANUEL de la CARIDAD
DOMINGO MACHADO
JOSEF GUERIERRES
LEONARDO GONZALEZ
TOMAS LOPEZ
LUIS CUARTEL
FRANCISCO CAMPOS
VALERIN RODRIGUEZ
FRANCISCO TRUXILLO
DOMINGO GARCIA
DOMINGO RIVAS
PEDRO GUIA
CHRISTOBAL MOLERO
FRANCISCO RAMIREZ
PEDRO HERNANDEZ
NICOLE TOLENTINO
JOSEF CUARRERO

MARIANO PADRON
JUAN PEREZ
JOSEF GONZALEZ
JULIAN LOPEZ
JOSEF de MESA
ANTONIO PEREZ
SEVASTIAN CASOLA
NICOLAS RAMOS
GASPAR ZERPA
DIEGO BELLIDO
MARCOS SANABRIA
MANUEL OLIVO
ANTONIO GONZALEZ
JOAQUIM GOMEZ
JOSEF de la RAMOS
LORENZO RODRIGUEZ
BERNARDO GONZALEZ
GERONIMO CAMBELO

JOSEF QUINTANA
MANUEL RAMOS
JOSEF OJEDA
ANTONIO de FLORES
JUAN QUINTANA
JUAN de la FUENTE
DIEGO ALFONSO
PEDRO HERNANDEZ CAVEZA
SANTIAGO MOLINA
FRANCISCO DOMINGUEZ
ANTONIO BANTA
MIGUEL RAMIREZ
CARLOS SUAREZ
TOMAS BENDALO
DIEGO BETANCOURT
FRANCISCO CARAVELLO
DOMINGO NUNEZ
MARIANO GRAS

Note: Four names on above list found torn and illegible, therefore omitted.

Source: En la seccion Papeles de Cuba se encuentran tres libros maestros del cargo de los donativos que se dan a las familias islenos que se establecieron en la nueva poblacion de "Terra de Bueyes", Galveztown y Senora de Galvez. Al principio de cado libro hay un indice con los nombres de los cabezas de familia.

TERRA de BUYES (TERRE-AUX-BOEUF)

INDEX
TERRE-AUX-BOEUF FAMILIES

ABREU, Andrea, 81
ACOSTA, Domingo, 81
ACOSTA, Juan de, 82
AGUILAR, Antonio Ramon, 81
ALFONSO, Diego, 83
ALFONSO, Juan Antonio, 81
ALFONSO, Phelipe Luis, 81
ALVAREZ, Francisco, 81
ANGEL, Juan, 82
ARMAS, Antonio de, 81
ARMAS, Francisco, de, 81
AUGUSTINO, Josef, 81
BANTA, Antonio, 83
BARCELONA, Francisco, 82
BARGAS, Augustin, Manuel, 81
BARGAS, Phelipe, 81
BARRERO, Pedro, 82
BARRIOS, juan de, 82
BARROSO, Antonio, 82
BELLIDO, Diego, 83
BENDALO, Tomas, 83
BERMUDEZ, Josef, 82
BETANCOURT, Diego, 83
CABRERA, Domingo Antonio, 82
CABRERA, Juan, 81
CALSINI, Pedro, 81
CAMBELO, Geronimo, 83
CAMPOS, Francisco, 82
CAPITAN, Augustin, 81
CARAVELLO, Augustin, 81
CARDENA, Alonsa, 82
CARIDAD, Manuel de la, 82
CARRERO, Christoval Lorenzo, 81
CASOLA, Sevastian, 83
CASTILLO, Geronimo, 82
CAVEZA, Pedro Hernandez, 83
CHOCHO, Guillermo Gonzalez, 82
COLLADO, Tomas, 82
CUARRERO, Josef, 82
CUARTEL, Luis, 82
CUBAS, Alonso de, 81
CYPRIAN, Antonio, 82
DELGADO, Vicente, 81
DIAZ, Antonio, 81
DIAZ, Bartolome, 82
DOMINGUEZ, Andres, 81
DUENAS, Diego, 81
DURAN, Gregoria, 82
ENRIQUEZ, Domingo, 81
ENRIQUEZ, Matia, 81
ERMANO, Josef, 81
ERNAZ, Gregoria, 81
ESPINO, Josef, 82
ESTEVES, Pablo, 82
ESTRADA, Nicolas, 82
FILANO, Josef, 82
FLORES, Antonio de, 83
FUENTE, Juan de la, 83
GARCIA, Domingo, 81, 82
GARCIA, Juan, 81
GARCIA, Manuel Francisco, 82
GOMEZ, Joaquim, 83
GONZALEZ, Antonio, 81, 83
GONZALEZ, Bernardo, 83
GONZALEZ, Domingo, 82
GONZALEZ, Josef Antonio, 81
GONZALEZ, Juan Antonio, 81
GONZALEZ, Luca, 82
GONZALEZ, Manuel, 81, 82
GRAN, Mariano, 81
GRAS, Mariano, 83
GUERIAO, Domingo Francisco, 81
GUERIDO, Francisco, 81
GUERIAO, Josef, 81
GUERIERRES, Josef, 82
GUIA, Pedro, 82
HERNANDEZ, Angel, 81
HERNANDEZ, Antonio, 82
HERNANDEZ, Bartolome, 81
HERNANDEZ, Domingo, 81
HERNANDEZ, Juan, 82
HERNANDEZ, Martin, 82
HERNANDEZ, Pedro, 82
HERNANDEZ, Nicolas, 81
HERRERA, Francisco, 82
HERRERA, Josef, 81
HERRERA, Juan Josef, 81
HERRERA, Lorenza Azepito, 82
LEON, Antono de, 82
LOPEZ, Julian, 83
LOPEZ, Lorenzo, 82
LOPEZ, Ramon, 82
LOPEZ, Tomas, 83

INDEX

TERRE-AUX-BOEUF FAMILIES

MACHADO, Domingo, 82
MACIAS, Luis, 82
MANISCO, Antonio, 82
MANNITO, Felipe Gonzales, 81
MAR, Francisco de la, 82
MARTIN, Josef, 82
MARTIN, Juan Antonio, 82
MARTIN, Mathias, 82
MARTIN, Miguel, 82
MARTIN, Pedro, 81
MARTINEZ, Josef Antonio, 82
MARZON, Francisco, 82
MEDERO, Juan, 81
MEDINO, Antonio, 82
MEDINO, Juan, Josef, 82
MELCHOR, Juan, 82
MELCHOR, Mauricio Garcia, 82
MELEAN, Francisco Sanchez, 82
MELEAN, Juan Sanchez, 82
MENDOZA, Christoval, 82
MERCEDES, Felipe, 82
MESA, Josef de, 83
MILAN, Salvador, 82
MOLERO, Christobal, 82
MOLINA, Santiago, 83
MONTESINO, Antonio, 81
MORALES, Diego, 82
MORALES, Josef, 82
MORALES, Juan, 81
MORALES, Juan Antonio, 82
MORALES, Ignacio, 81
MORALES, Maria, 81
MORALES, Pedro, 81
MORERO, Felix, 81
NAVARRO, Antonio Manuel, 82
NINA, Sebastiana de, 81
NOYA, Augustin Diaz de, 82
NUNEZ, Domingo, 82
NUNEZ, Manuel, 81
OJEDA, Christoval, 81
OJEDA, Josef, 83
OJEDA, Manuel, 81
OLIVO, Manuel, 83
ORTIZ, Gaspar, 81
PADRON, Mariano, 83
PAZ, Antonio de la, 82
PAZ, Ignacio de la, 81
PENA, Francisco, 82
PERERA, Josef, 82
PERERA, Roque Josef, 81
PERERA, Sebastian, 82
PEREZ, Antonio, 83
PEREZ, Josef Alesandro, 82
PEREZ, Juan, 81, 83
PEREZ, Manuel, 81
PESTANO, Antonio Garcia, 81
PHELIPE, Francisco, 81
PIMENTEL, Antonio, 82
PINO, Josef del, 82
PINTO, Augustin, 81
PLASCENCIA, Juan Manuel, 82
QUINTANA, Josef, 81
QUINTERO, Josef, 81
RAMIREZ, Antonio, 81
RAMIREZ, Christoval, 81
RAMIREZ, Diego, 81
RAMIREZ, Domingo, 82
RAMIREZ, Francisco, 82
RAMIREZ, Juan, 82
RAMIREZ, Salvador, 82
RAMOS, Domingo Miguel, 81
RAMOS, Gregorio, 81
REMEJO, Salvador Ermon, 81
REYES, Juan Antonio, 82
RIOS, Blas de, 81
RIVAS, Domingo, 82
RIVERO, Josef, 81
ROBERA, Josef, 82
RODRIGUEZ, Antonio, 82
RODRIGUEZ, Francisco, 82
RODRIGUEZ, Isidro, 81
RODRIGUEZ, Josef, 81
RODRIGUEZ, Juan Leon, 82
RODRIGUEZ, Valerin, 82
ROJAS, Josef Antonio de, 81
ROJAS, Nicolas de, 81
ROMERO, Josef, 82
ROMERO, Juan Ortiz, 81
ROMERO, Lorenzo 82
RUBIO, Antonio, 82
RUIZ, Josef Gonzalez, 81

TERRE-AUX-BOEUF FAMILIES

SAEA, Josef Enriquez, 81
SANABRIA, Marcos, 83
SANABRIA, Miguel, 83
SANCHEZ, Gaspar, 81
SANCHEZ, Joseph Perrera, 82
SANCHEZ, Juan Antonio, 82
SANDINO, Vicente, 82
SANTOS, Antonio, 82
SEGURA, Juan de, 81
SUAREZ, Carlos, 83
SUAREZ, Francisco, 82
SUAREZ, Josef, 81
SUAREZ, Juan, 81, 82
SUAREZ, Maria, 82

TOLEDO, Francisco, 81
TOLENTINO, Nicole, 82
TORRES, Juan de, 81
TRUXILLO, Francisco, 82

VENTURA, Christoval, 82
VIERA, Francisco, 81
VIERA, Josef, 81
VIERA, Juan, 81
VIERA, Salvador, 82

RECRUITS AND THEIR FAMILIES

WHO EMBARKED ON

JUNE 28, 1783

ON BOARD THE

"FRAGATA LLAMADA MARGARITA"

UNDER THE COMMAND OF

CAPTAIN DON FRANCISCO VARELA

JUNE 28, 1783

INFANTRY OF LOUISIANA

Account of the number of families and persons coming from the Canary Islands destined to the Province of Louisiana. They embarked and were sent to New Orleans on the "Fragata Llamada Margarita," under the command of Captain Don Francisco Varela.

FAMILIES	NUMBER	PERSONS
1	JUAN ALEMAN	1
1	FRANCISCO GARCIA ORAMUS	1
	FRANCESCA, his wife	1
	JOSEF, his son	1
	GERONIMO, his son	1
	MARCELINA, his daughter	1
1	GASPAR ZERPA	1
	ANA, his mother	1
	FRANCISCO, his brother	1
1	JOSEF y MESA	1
	JOSEFA, his wife	1
	MARIA, his daughter	1
1	FRANCISCO de la MAR	1
	MARGARITA, his wife	1
	JUAN, his son	1
	SEVASTIAN, his son	1
	ROSA, his daughter	1
	MARCELA, his daughter	1
	JUANA, his daughter	1
	DOMINGO, his son	1
1	MIGUEL SANABRIA	1
	CATHALINA, his wife	1
	MARIA, his daughter	1
1	DOMINGO de SOSA	1
1	ANTONIO PEREZ	1
	JOSEFA, his wife	1
	MARIA, his daughter	1
	JUAN, his son	1
1	NICOLAS FOLENTINO	1
	JUANA, his wife	1
	JOSEF, his son	1
	ANTONIO, his son	1
	MARIA, his daughter	1
	THOMASA, his sister	1
9		34

RECRUITS AND THEIR FAMILIES

WHO EMBARKED ON

AUGUST 7, 1783

ON BOARD THE

"SS TRINADAD"

UNDER THE COMMAND OF

CAPTAIN DON JUAN BORLA

AUGUST 7, 1783

INFANTRY REGIMENT OF LOUISIANA

Account of the number of families and persons coming from the Canary Islands destined to the Province of Louisiana. They embarked and were sent to New Orleans in a mail boat named "SS TRINADAD", under the command of Captain Don Juan Borla.

FAMILIES	NUMBER	PERSONS
1	THOMAS MENESER	1
	JOSEFA, his wife	1
	ANTONIO, his son	1
1	JUAN RAMIREZ	1
	UNA, his wife	1
1	CHRISTOVAL LUIS MOLERO	1
	JOSEFA, his wife	1
	BARTOME, his son	1
	JUAN	1
	ANTONIA, his daughter	1
	AUGUSTINA, his daughter	1
	MARIA, his daughter	1
	CATHARINA, his daughter	1
	FRANCISCO, his son	1
1	FRANCISCO RAMIREZ	1
	MARIA, his wife	1
	JOSEF, his son	1
	JUAN, his son	1
	BERNARDO, his son	1
	MARIA, his son	1
1	DOMINGO GONZALEZ	1
	CATHARINA, his wife	1
	JUAN, his son	1
	MIGUEL, his son	1
	BARTOME, his son	1
	JUAN, his son	1
	MARIA, his daughter	1
1	JOSEF AUGUSTIN MARTIN	1
	MARIA, his wife	1
	A daughter	1
6	TOTAL	30

FAMILIES	NUMBER	PERSONS
Brought Forward 9		34
1	NICOLAS ESTRADA	1
1	DOMINGO RAMOS	1
	GABRIELLA, his wife	1
	ROSA, daughter	1
	MARIA, daughter	1
	JUANA, daughter	1
	ANTONIA, daughter	1
	MARIA, daughter	1
1	MARCOS SANABRIA	1
	JUANA, his daughter	1
1	PETRONA, WIDOW OF BARTOMO RODRIGUEZ	1
	MANUEL, her son	1
	DOMINGO, her son	1
	ANTONIO, her son	1
	MARIA, her daughter	1
1	PEDRO HERNANDEZ	1
	THOMASOSA, his wife	1
	FRANCESCA, his daughter	1
	JOSEFA, his daughter	1
	PEDRO, his son	1
	FRANCISCO, his son	1
	JUAN, his son	1
1	PEDRO GIA	1
	VICENTE, his son	1
	PEDRO, his son	1
	ANTONIA, his daughter	1
1	ANTONIO JOSEF de LEON	1
	AUGUSTINA, his wife	1
	CATHARINA, his daughter	1
	ANTONIA, his daughter	1
1	LEONARDO GONZALEZ	1
	CATHARINA, his wife	1
	ANTONIO, his son	1
	JOSEF, his son	1
1	DOMINGO MANTO	1
	JOSEFA, his wife	1
	FELIPE, his son	1
18		81

FAMILIES	NUMBER	PERSONS
Brought Forward 18		81
1	GERONIMO CURBETO	1
	EUGENIA, his wife	1
	AUGUSTO, his son	1
	FRANCISCO, his son	1
1	FRANCISCO LUIS HERNANDEZ	1
	JOSEFA, his wife	1
	JOSEF, his son	1
	FRANCESCA, his daughter	1
1	JUAN PEREZ	1
	ISABEL, his wife	1
1	DOMINGO AMARO	1
	JOSEF, his son	1
	LUIS, his son	1
1	JOSEF BAYONO	1
	THOMASO, his son	1
	MARIA, his daughter	1
	EUGENIA, his daughter	1
1	BARTOME PEREZ	1
	ANA, his wife	1
	JOSEF, his son	1
	FRANCISCO, his son	1
	MARIA, his daughter	1
24		103

"FRAGATA LLAMADA MARGARITA" AND THE "SS TRINADAD"

ALEMAN, Josef, 88
AMARO, Domingo, 92
AMARO, Luis, 92

BAYONA, Eugenia, 92
BAYONA, Josef, 92
BAYONA, Maria, 92
BAYONA, Thomasa, 92
BORLA, Don Juan, 90

CURBETO, Augusto, 92
CURBETO, Eugenia, 92
CURBETO, Francisco, 92
CURBETO, Geronimo, 92

ESTRADA, Nicolas, 91

FOLENTINO, Antonio, 88
FOLENTINO, Josef, 88
FOLENTINO, Juana, 88
FOLENTINO, Maria, 88
FOLENTINO, Nicolas, 88
FOLENTINO, Thomasa, 88

GONZALEZ, Antonio, 88, 91
GONZALEZ, Bartome, 90
GONZALEZ, Catharina, 90, 91
GONZALEZ, Domingo, 90
GONZALEZ, Josef, 91
GONZALEZ, Juan, 90
GONZALEZ, Juana, 90
GONZALEZ, Leonardo, 91
GONZALEZ, Maria, 90
GONZALEZ, Miguel, 90

HERNANDEZ, Francesca, 91, 92
HERNANDEZ, Francisco, 91
HERNANDEZ, Francisco Luis, 92
HERNANDEZ, Josef, 92
HERNANDEZ, Josefa, 91, 92
HERNANDEZ, Juan, 91
HERNANDEZ, Pedr, 91
HERNANDEZ, Pedr, Jr., 91
HERNANDEZ, Thomasosa, 91

GIA, Antonia, 91
GIA, Pedro, 91
GIA, Pedro, Jr., 91
GIA, Vicente, 91

LEON, Antonio de, 91
LEON, Antonia de, 91
LEON, Augustina de, 91
LEON, Catharina de, 91

MANTO, Domingo, 91
MANTO, Felipe, 91
MANTO, Josefa, 91
MAR, Domingo de la, 81
MAR, Francisco de la, 81
MAR, Juan de la, 81
MAR, Juana de la, 81
MAR, Marcela de la, 81
MAR, Margarita de la, 81
MAR, Rosa de la, 81
MAR, Sevastian de la, 81
MARTIN, Josef Augustin, 90
MARTIN, Maria, 90
MENESER, Antonio, 90
MENESER, Josefa, 90
MENESER, Tomas, 90
MOLERO, Antonio, 90
MOLERO, Augustina, 90
MOLERO, Bartome, 90
MOLERO, Catharina, 90
MOLERO, Christoval Luis, 90
MOLERO, Josefa, 90
MOLERO, Juan, 90
MOLERO, Maria, 90

ORAMUS, Francesca, 88
ORAMUS, Francisco Garcia, 88
ORAMUS, Geronimo, 88
ORAMUS, Josef, 88
ORAMUS, Marcelina, 88

PEREZ, Ana, 92
PEREZ, Antonio, 88
PEREZ, Bartome, 92
PEREZ, Francisco, 92
PEREZ, Isabel, 89
PEREZ, Josefa, 88
PEREZ, Juan, 88, 92
PEREZ, Maria, 88, 92

RAMIREZ, Bernardo, 90
RAMIREZ, Francisco, 90
RAMIREZ, Juan, 90

INDEX

"FRAGATA LLAMADA MARGARITA" AND THE "SS TRINADAD"

RAMIREZ, Maria, 90
RAMIREZ, Una, 90
RODRIGUEZ, Antonio, 91
RODRIGUEZ, Domingo, 91
RODRIGUEZ, Maria, 91
RODRIGUEZ, Manuel, 91

SANABRIA, Cathalina, 88
SANABRIA, Juana, 91
SANABRIA, Marcos, 91
SANABRIA, Miguel, 88

ZERPA, Ana, 88
ZERPA, Gaspar, 88
ZERPA, Francisco, 88

www.ingramcontent.com/pod-product-compliance
Lightning Source LLC
Chambersburg PA
CBHW071137280326
41935CB00010B/1259
9780806305226